SUPERVIVENCIA

MIGUEL ALGARIN

EDITED BY
MARC NEWELL

INTRODUCTION BY
ERNESTO QUIÑONEZ

Arte Público Press
Houston, Texas

Survival Supervivencia is made possible through grants from the City of Houston through the Houston Arts Alliance, and by the Exemplar Program, a program of Americans for the Arts in Collaboration with the LarsonAllen Public Services Group, funded by the Ford Foundation.

Recovering the past, creating the future

Arte Público Press
University of Houston
452 Cullen Performance Hall
Houston, Texas 77204-2004

Photography by Shirley Miranda-Rodriguez, Somos Arte
Cover design by Somos Arte/www.somosarte.com

Algarin, Miguel.
    Survival Supervivencia / by Miguel Algarin; edited by Marc Newell ; introduction by Ernesto Quiñonez.
        p.   cm.
    ISBN 978-1-55885-541-0 (alk. paper)
    I. Newell, Marc. II. Title.
    PS3551.L359S87 2009
    811'.54—dc22

                                                2008048549
                                                      CIP

9 0 1 2 3 4 5 6 7 8   10 9 8 7 6 5 4 3 2 1

ACKNOWLEDGMENTS

To

MARC NEWELL
my editor

ARCOS COMMUNICATIONS

MARIE DENISE JEAN-LOUIS

NICOLÁS KANELLOS

VILMA, ISABEL AND JULIO
my Rutgers University friends

CONTENTS

INTRODUCTION

When I was in high school I was led to believe a poet had to be dead or close to it. My head was filled with images of crusty, old, white men like Robert Frost, writing verse. The places these poets spoke about were far away and though I felt a sensitivity toward words, something told me these poets were ignoring me and my parents. Then one day by sheer luck, while browsing the Aguilar Public Library's shelves, I came upon a book of poems that spoke to me. This book told me that when a people lack representation then that's when it's time for them to create their own mythology. The mainland Puerto Ricans were absent in literature, they appeared in a few footnotes but there was nothing there claiming them as part of the grand scheme of letters. And so, it was time to invent, to create what Miguel Algarin called the "Newness," a brand new mythology overflowing with its own codes, terminology, laws, and thus, the Nuyorican was born.

For me *Nuyorican Poetry: An Anthology of Puerto Rican Words and Feelings* edited by Miguel Algarin and Miguel Piñero, (William Morrow & Co, 1975), was as profound as any religious experience. The elation I felt seeing that my neighborhood of Spanish Harlem, and Miguel Algarin's beloved Loisaida were valid material for literature was like an epiphany striking me. That the voices, the gestures, the Spanglish, the stories of a people I knew so well, were as worthy and as legitimate as any found in Anglo letters was a revelation. I recall not sitting but reading all the poems standing. The poems were as funny as they were sad. But it was more than that, I was terrified because I knew then that with talent, will and a good sense of storytelling I might one day grow to be a writer. There were no more excuses, Miguel Algarin, Miguel Piñero, Lucky CienFuegos, Sandra María Esteves, Pedro Pietri, Bimbo Rivas, Shorty Bon Bon had opened up a new mythmaking factory. They were telling America and American letters, "since you give us no significance, we are breaking away from the tribe." These poems, these early performance poems, were the Nuyorican's constitution. They were our own myths, our own language, as Miguel Algarin stated, being born out of two cultures clashing into one another. The "Newness" had arrived, it was real and it had accepted me, it understood me and I wanted in.

Flash forward a few years ahead to a skinny kid at The City College of New York writing bad stories about El Barrio. The stories were bad because the skinny kid had not understood everything that Miguel Algarin's poems were telling him. And that was that talent, will and a good sense of storytelling is not enough to truly capture a people who lack representation. If I wanted to be part of the Nuyorican mythmaking machine, I had better have an abundance of love and compassion not just for the model Nuyorican, but for all. Miguel Algarin's poems humanize, they continue to elevate some of the most most deprived, cold-blooded, HIV-infected, lost, love-starved, poverty-stricken bottom feeders that populate our communities. Miguel Algarin's poems are pages of compassion and understanding, like Baldwin's Sonny's Blues, they teach me that I, too, can love a junky. I, too, am his brother. My early East Harlem stories were bad because I had not yet grasped this fact. I was not listening to what Miguel Algarin's poems were telling me, that by humanizing the seemingly inhuman you are thereby humanizing the reader. My early stories were accurate but loveless and if I wanted to write about a people, my people, who lack representation and therefore need their own myths, I would now have to start from scratch. Love Is Hard Work.

Few capture, few convey this love, this suffering of a people like Miguel Algarin does in his poems: the hallucinations of a junky, the peaceful quenching feeling of a hit, the ache of junk sickness, the rage of sexual claustrophobia, the choking fear of HIV, the nausea of its cocktails, the tightening screws of paranoia, the lure of easy street and its petty drugs, the loneliness of the poet. Miguel Algarin dives down into an urban underclass, he gets inside their skin, burrowing his feelings and when he comes up for air, he stuns us with empathy. We learn that the new myths he is creating are codifying: that in the end, there is hope for the hopeless and love for the loveless.

Survival Supervivencia is a collection of some of Miguel Algarin's best known poems along with essays and recollections. The essay "Nuyorican Language" from the anthology that changed my way of thinking, is reprinted here to my joy and delight. The essay is the ultimate political urbane statement on survival. It was published in 1975, and what strikes me most is how the essay holds well in today's age of gentrification, for Miguel Algarin saw it coming, "To stay free is not theoretical. It is to take over your immediate environment. . ." I am proud to confess that much of "Nuyorican Language" is incorporated in the long-winded speeches that my character Willie Bodega of *Bodega Dreams* recites like a broken record. Also included in this collection are famous poems like "A Mongo Affair," "Always throw the first punch," "Ray Barretto: December 4, 1976," "Christmas Eve: Nuyorican Café," "On Seeing Miky's Body's," "Sunday, August 11, 1974" are here and doing as well as Miguel Algarin himself, who is alive and will be among us for a very, very long time.

Survival Supervivencia is quintessential Algarin, fueled by poems that take the reader to the Nuyorican struggle: to stay frosty, to stay cool and to love one another. These poems document the existence of a people who America systematically yanked out of their beloved Puerto Rico and promised them everything and gave them nothing but welfare, rats and roaches. A people who had to create themselves from zero, a people who to this day continue to evolve. Miguel Algarin's poems are also here to remind us that America is corrupt and that we reject its myths of Paul Bunyan, Mickey Mouse and the Kennedys. We will not buy into the American Dream because by its own definition it is destructive for it does not nurture, it does not entail all those beautiful things that are truly important: truth, integrity and a genuine love for the dejected.

We, the Nuyorican from New York, the Philarican from Philadelphia, the Chicarican from Chicago, the Larican from Los Angeles, the entire Puerto Rican population born or raised on the mainland as well as all of our Latino brothers and sisters and anyone else who wishes to tag along, will create our own myths, our own language, a "Newness" where we will love the unlovable. Miguel Algarin's poems are here to reduce it all to its bare bones, to tell us:

> The struggle is really simple
> I will be born
> I will not be taught how to behave
> I will not make my muscles vestigial
> I will not digest myself

> *Ernesto Quiñonez*
> *Ithaca, April 18, 2008*

Survival
(1978)

the struggle is really simple
i was born
i was taught how to behave
i was shown how to accommodate—
i resist being humanized
into feelings not my own—
the struggle is really simple
i will be born
i will not be taught how to behave
i will not make my muscles vestigial
i will not digest myself

NUYORICAN LANGUAGE
(1975)

Introduction for *Nuyorican Poetry:*
An Anthology of Puerto Rican Words and Feelings

For the poor New York Puerto Rican, there are three survival possibilities. The first is to labor for money and exist in eternal debt. The second is to refuse to trade hours for dollars and to live by your will and "hustle." The third possibility is to create alternative behavioral habits. It is here that the responsibilities of the poet start, for there are no "alternatives" without a vocabulary in which to express them. The poet is responsible for inventing the newness. The newness needs words—words never heard before or used before. The poet has to invent a new language—a new tradition of communication.

The first choice: my mother and father arrive at a feeling of safety when they find themselves dutifully employed to a Mr. Frisk or the Goldwater Memorial Hospital that provides them with a salary. María, my mother, has been working ever since I was born, and she plans to keep on working. She feels safe when she works. She feels proud. She is entitled to honor herself and her husband and her children. María is eager to live. For many years she cut leather for handbags to be sent to Miami for sale in luxury hotels. María was so responsible, so fast, so thorough, so on time that she always got whatever overtime there was. Her boss, Mr. Frisk, loved her. He even tried to seduce her, but María was virtuous. At last, she felt the need to leave; I never knew why, but she moved her HOURS elsewhere. Once María found a job in the dietary department at the Goldwater Memorial Hospital, she was determined to climb the ladder. She set out to compete. She took on the night shift: 4:00 a.m. to 2:30 p.m. She never missed a day. She became assistant to the assistant of the Head Assistant Dietician. She worked with precision during many crises. She is now assistant to the Head Assistant Dietician. María's hours are still the same. She goes in rain, snow or sleet. She is important in every way—but her take-home pay is only $135.00 a week. Her live planet hours have been richly worked but very poorly paid. She is into the tense struggle of keeping housed, clothed and fed. She lives in eternal debt. She works to survive without embarrassment.

The second possibility is living by risks—risks of all types. There are people who will comply with a renegade's law: cheat, lie, strike, kill, deal, sell, buy, rob, cut, choke. Once there is no respect for the system, the options are numerous but very dangerous. Many rules establish the field of action that is permitted. Whenever one of these rules is broken, there is serious institutional action taken against the offender. You can either comply with the law or grab the moment. Take over a building. Go downtown and argue for the deed of ownership. The Renigades of Harlem are doing it. They risk having to learn how to pipe a building, how to gut it, how to build a roof. They risk in order to construct the life that is happening to them. The second choice of refusing to trade live hours for dollars is a choice of endless varieties. The streets are where the game is played. The consequences of street games are totally unpredictable. If you get caught, you must pay. It is true that when you get caught there are plenty of people involved in the same act as you. Yet the fact is that you (not the other) got caught. You become an example—a correctional threat to those not caught. In other words, the second choice is to get out there on the streets and "juggle" without getting caught. Joey's mother struggles with raising a family by selling food in the park. John hustles coke. Meanwhile the street cliques are involved in a transition from organized street hustling to coordinated alternative street government.

The poet blazes a path of fire for the self. He juggles with words. He lives risking each moment. Whatever he does, in every way he moves; he is a prince of the inner-city jungle. He is the philosopher of the sugar cane that grows between the cracks of concrete sidewalks. The poet studies Che, Don Pedro Albizu Campos, Mao. He carries the tension of the streets in his mind and he knows how to execute his mind in action. The past teaches the young to juggle all the balls at the same time. The poet juggles with every street corner east of First Avenue and south of Fourteenth Street ending at the Brooklyn Bridge. Poetry is the full act of naming. Naming states of mind. The rebellious, the contentious, the questioning personality wins out. And poetry is on the street burning it up with its visions of the times to be:

> Now only our tomorrows
> Will tell if that arrow
> of love with a head
> of art penetrates into
> higher dimensions.
>
> ("Sad Will Be The Nights If The Planets Will No Longer Shine"
> by Lucky CienFuegos)

The poet sees his function as a troubadour. He tells the tale of the streets to the streets. The people listen. They cry, they laugh, they dance as the troubadour opens up and times his voice and moves his pitch and rhythm to the high tension of "*bomba*" truth. Proclamations of hurt, of anger and hatred. Whirls of high-pitched singing. The voice of the street poet must amplify itself. The poet pierces the crowd with cataracts of clear, clean, precise, concrete words about the liquid, shifting latino reality around him.

Ismael Rivera is "*el sonero major*" at Joey's house. "The troubadour among troubadours" is the man who sings the live sweat pulse of a people. Ismael's words are about the island, his mother-in-law, his love, life. Ismael is Nuyorican rhythmic communication. Stripped, Ismael is the clean, unspoiled voice of Puerto Ricans both in New York City and the island of Puerto Rico. He is the passionate historian of both worlds. His record sets the tone of Joey's mother's two birthday parties in one. Latin music presides. Everybody dances. The eyes of those who sit dance. The room is in motion. Exhausted factory muscles ripen into joy. Children watch. The sawed-off dungarees, bobby socks, beach caps and lightly shaded shades move nonstop. Beer everywhere. Nuyorican life goes on in spite of the eternal debt for which there is an eternal hustle. Joey's sister is dressed in black on platform shoes. She spins. She moves to the joy of her own birthday. Joey's mother passes colder-than-cold beer. I am settled. The record changes. The rhythm is Pacheco now. The children see everything. The risk is total involvement. The party costs as much as it costs. The need is to meet the cost and get into debt wherever necessary. A birthday party must be celebrated. Joey's mother spent her actual cash on the cake. She took the beer from la bodega on credit, potato chips provided by her sister, candles for the cake left from last year except for six that Muñeca brought with her. Joey's mother plans to sell "*frituras*" on Sundays to make up the money. She is nowadays a little afraid of the park because she was robbed last week. Nevertheless, she'll make up this debt. The party has to be paid for because she'll need to do it again next year. She lives by risks, and that means that she might be caught. Getting caught means getting arrested in the park for selling "*frituras*." If arrested, she'll be removed from the flow of street life. However, to risk and not get caught is the law of the street. Most people manage it. Joey's mother is risking it all.

To stay free is not theoretical. It is to take over your immediate environment. Who owns the building in which you live? Find him out, then deal directly. Who is willing to talk his way through the legalese that puts wrinkles on the tongue? Roberto Nazario is willing. He can chew a Municipal Housing Authority contract right down to its bold deceits. So let's take it by steps. If you do not settle for selling your hours for pay, then you must juggle. If you juggle, you can do it for the moment. But there are juggling acts that can stick beyond the day's rip-off. The Renigades of Harlem, an upper Manhattan street clique, are juggling with contractors, electricians, plumbers. They learn skills as the needs make themselves felt, so that as the work on the building grows, so do the native skills of the members of the Renigades. Roberto is on the streets night and day supplying information: where do I get a plumber, an electrician, a plasterer? He always knows. He works in the Lower East Side, but he learns in East Harlem. The energies are dispersed, but the effort to collect them is on. The alternative is the doing. The Dynamite Brothers (a lower East Side clique) rehabilitate their adopted building. They will do whatever is necessary to own, manage and repair the dwelling. Roberto, in turn, will chew on a mountain of legal conceits like a rabbit on a giant carrot.

But struggle is a hustle, and the struggle-hustle is experienced as a shifting balance. Sometimes you can get away with it, other times you get caught. Sometimes you drive for a week without a license, and then you get stopped because the rear lights are out; and then you get two tickets in one throw. Sometimes, a Dynamite Brother can pull a series of hold-ups and get away, yet doing the next—the easiest pull-off—he gets caught. Roberto is saying legalize your "risks." If you protect your community, he says, it will defend you when you need it. If you threaten the community, it will turn you in. People who build their own housing will want to protect it. Roberto sees this clearly. Communities are united by small actions that return the law to the people and inspire them to trust each other.

The rehabilitation of a building on East Second Street by the Dynamites awakens the respect of the people who see the clique at work day to day. You survive by examples. You survive in the doing. You survive by gut will. If the Dynamites defend the people, the people will love and respect their right to establish the LAWS of the community.

Laws control behavior. But it is a choice that people make. If laws destroy a community's sense of safety, then the laws are not purposeful—not if they make people vulnerable rather than strong.

A clique (a New York street clique) is a group of people who offer each other safety. Safety in numbers is nationalism. Nationalism is mutual protection. The clique can be small or large. Large nationalist cliques (ITT, Dupont, Chase Manhattan Bank) protect and define their laws. A small nationalist clique is any city gang that is geographically located in a particular neighborhood or city block and protects its laws. The purpose for wearing colors, designing a flag, or having an anthem is to develop an identity. A city clique needs to have a geographical identity as inviolable as that of any nation formally recognized by the UN. But above all, a clique offers protection and a sense of "national safety" for its immediate members. Once survival, street protection, is shared by a group of men and women, the next step is to assert their collective will again and again and again. Roberto teaches that to adopt a building is the next elementary concrete collective gesture to make.

Work together, and paranoia will be diluted. The Dynamite Brothers meet the Renigades of Harlem, and the message is work. The mood is humble. Logy, Supreme Vice-President of the Renigades of Harlem, speaks about the commitment to build. The Renigade Brothers perceive the will that has brought the Dynamite Brothers to 119th Street. There is a force—a pull to cohere. Chocolate, a Dynamite, speaks from his guts because he, when in need, finds help without fear among the Renigades. Shorty speaks about taking over the fate of the Puerto Rican in the city. Roy, Supreme President, speaks about having started the Renigades in 1972. He talks about the growth of consciousness from street clubhouse rumbles to concrete decisions about rehabilitating buildings. Roy explains how the police didn't think there would be enough ingenuity. But a chute came up. The dirt, bricks, metal, debris came tumbling down. The police ridiculed the idea. The police doubted, doubted, doubted. They doubted beyond doubt:

"They can't do it—they don't know how." But the fact is that the Renigades can now teach the Dynamites how to hustle in the housing survival struggle.

Logy's logic is simple. The Dynamites put work into the building and the rewards for the work are clear: clean, warm, secure housing owned by the Dynamites. No landlord, no check going out to management agencies that do not provide the services they are charging for. Logy speaks the Shaman wisdom of our city tribes. Supreme Vice-President Logy speaks the words of a visionary. Logy is a poet of action. His metaphysics is to do and then see the consequences. His clear, clean pride in what he is doing arouses the purest impulses in the Dynamites. Everybody feels the simple love and truth in him—the Supreme Vice-President of the Government of the Streets. The marriage is on the way, and 119th Street has married Second Street and the results are a possible coalition government: The Dynamite Renigades.

The next day, the Renigades continue their work, and the Dynamites initiate their construction. The work at first is slow and there is no existing language to express the feelings and work to be done. Language and action are simultaneous realities. Actions create the need for verbal expression. If the action is new, so must the words that express it come through as new. Newness in language grows as people do and learn things never done or learned before. The experience of Puerto Ricans on the streets of New York has caused a new language to grow: Nuyorican. Nuyoricans are a special experience in the immigration history of the city of New York. We come to the city as citizens and can retain the use of Spanish and include English. The "naturalizing" process for citizenship does not scare the average Nuyorican into learning English. But pressures of getting a job stimulate the need to master a minimal English usage. But really, it is the English around you that seeps into your vocabulary. Everything is in English in the USA, yet there is also a lot of Spanish, and Spanish is now gaining. The mixture of both languages grows. The interchange between both yields new verbal possibilities, new images to deal with the stresses of living on tar and cement.

There is at the edge of every empire a linguistic explosion that results from the many multilingual tribes that collect around wealth and power. The Nuyorican is a slave class that trades hours for dollars at the lowest rung of the earning scale. The poems in this anthology document the conditions of survival: many roaches many busts, many drug poems, many hate poems—many, many poems of complaints. But the complaints are delivered in a new rhythm. It is a *bomba* rhythm with many changing pitches delivered with a bold stress. The pitches vary, but the stress is always *bomba* and the vocabulary is English and Spanish mixed into a new language. The power of Nuyorican talk is that it is street rooted. It is the way people talk in the raw before the spirit is molded into "standards." Any Nuyorican mother shopping for food in La Marqueta on 115th Street is capable of delivering herself of beautiful, original talk:

1) dame half pound de chuleta
2) aceite, bacon, una matita de recao y un container de leche
3) un momento Mister, no speak to me de esa manera

Nuyorican is full of muscular expression. It is a language full of short, pulsating rhythms that manifest the unrelenting strain that the Nuyorican experiences.

Communications between Nuyoricans and the city institutions are very strained. It is mostly caused by distrust. Language breaks down easily between institutions and those laying claims on change and newfound strength. Step by step, trust can be found. But it is not a balanced trust. It goes on and off: for example, Deputy Fire Chief John Hart is in the East Second Street firehouse protecting himself and his company from a City Hall investigation about a woman who died in a fire on Fifth Street. The company stands at attention. The Dynamite Brothers are standing outside. Deputy Fire Chief Hart wants to know how it came to be that "the woman's apartment blew up in flames after the fire had been tamed?" We are listening and the paranoia level rises as the firehouse lieutenant asks for privacy. First, the large mobile door is lowered. We then knock on the office door. A burly, rude lieutenant growls, "Go away, come back later, just go away." Slam! We wait. We are angered and humiliated. But we wait. We wait for the Deputy Fire Chief. We discuss storming the place, stringing the Fire Chief out of the fifth floor on rotted cotton candy rope. We feel the pressure to fight. But we wait. We wait courteously. After a long time, the deputy comes out. We had waited, and now is our chance.

Kool: May we have a word with you.
Deputy: What do you want?
Kool: We want to talk with you.
Deputy: Please give your complaints to the Firehouse
          Captain.
Kool: We're not here complaining; we want to discuss
          some things with you and your men.

The fire bells go off. Everybody moves. The Deputy Fire Chief has to go. But he makes a date with us. The time is set for six-thirty the same day. We agree. Later, we are asked to go to a meeting elsewhere so we change the time to six-thirty the next day.

We arrive. We have been talking a good part of the day, both about the lot down the street that we want to make into a park and the meeting with the Deputy Fire Chief. We know we are in two worlds. Deputy Fire Chief Hart speaks English. We speak Nuyorican. But we're ready to move to a point of understanding. The first fireman to speak warns us just to be "out there" and "open," to come out with all our grievances: "Just let it out, come out and name your complaints." One of the Dynamites says, "We're not in for a long rap about what we've done." The first fireman insists that "We have to have it out in the open." The Dynamite repeats that "The hostility between us is not the point of this meeting. We are here to discuss a needed change in our relationship with Chief Hart. The Dynamite Brothers are ready to work with the firemen, but we need their help in return. We are not here to complain." The worry wrinkles fall off each fireman's face. Chief Hart looks astonished. But we know that trust between us goes on and off. One of the Dynamites says, "We would like to acquire legal possession of the lot down the street. We are willing to clean it up. We could use your help." Nuyorican and English are running neck to neck. Both sides are being respected. The feelings of both parties are not in static. We are feeling balanced. The Dynamites and the firemen move into a coherence. Chief Hart looks at Captain Docherty. He snaps into recollection, "That's the lot the city offered us for a parking lot, but we never got to make use of it." The Chief looks pleased. One of the firemen consents to pitch in and work. All of the firemen finally join in consent.

Two languages have met. We talked and understood each other. The outlaw meets the institution. The outlaw discovers the community needs him! "Our fighting is over, and our work has just begun." This news I bring you may be hard to believe, but the day has come where the Dynamite Brothers and Sisters are here to help." (From *A Letter To The Community* by Kool, Supreme President of the Dynamites.) The community feels the change. The people's trust grows as the news travels. The need for finding safety is always present. The Dynamites' new image sends vibrations of goodwill throughout the neighborhood. Kool's announcement has traveled through every apartment on the block.

> We will protect your homes, your stores—protect them from being robbed. We will protect your kids from getting in trouble like the ones we were in. We will stop violence among ourselves. What I mean is that you (the community) should trust in us so that we can trust in you.

A new day is born.

A new day needs a new language, or else the day becomes a repetition of yesterday. Invention is not always a straightening up of things. Oftentimes, the newness disrupts. It causes chaos. Two languages coexisting in your head as modes of expression can either strengthen alertness or cause confusion. The streets resound with Spanish and English. The average Nuyorican has a working command of both and normally uses both languages simultaneously. Ordinary life for the Nuyorican happens in both languages. The factory laborer reads instructions in English but feels in Spanish. Thus, he expresses responses to the conditions of his environment in Nuyorican. The standardization of a street-born language is always perilous and never easy. Around existing, formally recognized languages, whole empires of rules grow. Rules and regulations about speech are conventions that grow (at first) as patterns of self-expression which become fixed by usage—so that as all of the rules and regulations that spring from street usage become established patterns, a body of "grammatical rules" will correspondingly evolve. The evolution of a grammar is slow and at first always a suspicious process for two reasons. The first is that a language that grows out of street experience is dynamic and erratic. There are no boundaries around it. There were no boundaries around the languages that came together in the Iberian peninsula many centuries ago. It took English a good thousand years to establish itself as a formal, regulated tongue. It takes time to have disruptive, tense, informal street talk arrive at an organized respectability. Nuyorican is at its birth. English nouns function as verbs. Spanish verbs function as adjectives. Spanish and English words are made to serve the tenses of existence. Raw life needs raw verbs and raw nouns to express the action and to name the quality of experience. It is necessary to guard against the pressure to legitimize a street language that is in its infancy. Imposing a system of usage on Nuyorican would at the present time stunt its childhood and damage its creative intuition.

The second problem in evolving rules around Nuyorican speech patterns is that if they do not legitimately arise from the street people, the rules and regulations will come from outside, already existing grammatical patterns that are not new but old systems of rules imposed on new patterns of speech. This will not do.

The risk is on. The Nuyorican will have to continue to express himself without "legitimate rules" to govern his speech. We have to admit that speech comes first. We first verbalize the stresses of street experience and then later, in the aftermath of our street survival, we will sit and talk of our newness and how to shape it.

> Get rid of the fruit that is spoiled
> before it rubs off on freshness.
>> (Starling, the cook at Project R.E.T.U.R.N.)

July 1975
Nuyorican Village
New York City

THE POLITICS OF POETRY
(1976)

for Pablo Neruda's *Song of Protest*

I. EVENTS

When I was a child, I trusted my mother completely. Whenever she felt safe, I felt safe. I remember looking out for my mother's signals. I was always alert for signals of fear. I always looked to my parents to explain how things worked, and they always responded to my questions. Luis Muñoz Marín was governor of Puerto Rico when I was a child. I remember how once my brother and sister were held up above the head of the crowd to see Luis Muñoz Marín exit from a radio station where he had been making a speech. My mother was filled with electrical joy. My father stood gently still and full of pride. But I was very sad because my uncle had decided that I was too fat to sit on his shoulders. As the governor exited, a furious clapping of hands was heard. So exciting was the clapping that I forgot my sadness and began to applaud, though all I could see were his polished white shoes.

I remember how much respect the whole family had for Mr. Muñoz Marín. Once, there was a bloody fight between my Uncle Benitín and our next-door neighbor who kept insisting that Mr. Muñoz Marín was selling us out. It was a puzzling experience. I had never seen my Uncle Benitín so nettled. It was as if a bee had stung him and he couldn't shake the pain. Uncle Benitín leaped at the man's throat and tried to kill him. Both families ran to the rescue; the men were separated and everybody cooled down, but the men never spoke to each other again. Overall, Mr. Muñoz Marín was, however, much more loved and respected than detested.

My family moved to New York City, so Mr. Muñoz Marín faded into the background of my mind as the new environment began to dominate my senses. I thought about the island, but its leaders and its politics left my memory's sight. Feelings about the past were encouraged, but not on the bad side. All that the family ever talked about when they got together were the good times. Rarely were the painful times brought up. A very mellow and partially ideal image of the past began to develop.

I had to cope with myself on the streets of New York before I could concentrate on the historical events that had been or were developing in Puerto Rico. I focused my entire attention on New York until I learned to survive. Soon, however, I felt dissatisfied. It was not enough to have the new. I needed a history as well. I needed my memories, and for that I needed Spanish back. I looked to the Caribbean and South American writers to feed me feelings so that I could tap my faded memory.

It was then that I found Pablo Neruda's *Song of Protest*. I was on the prowl for clear images. It had become clearer to me that Mr. Muñoz Marín was not a shining knight. But my questions about him at home flustered and after a while embarrassed and demoralized the family. I stopped asking, but in Mr. Neruda, I found a teacher-friend. He wanted to tell me the events. He wanted to tell the truth so clearly that the poems he wrought are communications that seep into the neurological cells and nourish by arousing and nurturing the memory. Neruda's verbal images are chemical messages that change the body's composition.

It was really simple. I was looking to be taught, and Neruda wanted to teach, and as soon as I found Neruda, I brought him home:

> There is a fat worm in these waters
> in these lands a predatory worm:

he ate the island's flag
hoisting up his overseer's banner,
he was nourished from the captive blood
of the poor buried patriots.

("Muñoz Marín," II)

"'A fat worm'—that's a corrupted image from a corrupted poet," my Uncle Al shouted. The struggle was not easy. The reaction at home was definitive, "The poet of these poems is forgetting the business of poetry." My Uncle Al was aroused to aggression. I remember that he swung at me, flipping the table, the book, and me onto the floor. I kept insisting that it was "only a poem," and he shouted at me that it wasn't just a poem—that it was the devil trying to destroy the image of a good and righteous ruler. I was hurt and glad at Uncle Al's response. It was clear that Neruda's poems were hitting right smack in the middle of Uncle Al's stored-up pain. I stopped reading for that day.

I have heard poems read in public that have been praised for their beauty and structure but which cease to provoke responses beyond a few minutes after they are read. Not so with the poems in *Song of Protest*. These poems remain in action long after their reading is over. Neruda planned it that way:

On the golden crown of American wheat
the worm grew fat in a maggot heap
prospering in the monied shade,
bloodied with tortures and soldiers,
inaugurating false monuments,
making the native soil inherited
by their fathers an enslaved clod,
making an island as transparent as a star
into a small grave for slaves . . .

("Muñoz Marín," II)

There were no names too sacred or too powerful to reveal. Neruda was conscious of his task. He had set out to infuse with life the historical events of the last fifty years. Even if it meant disillusioning whole generations of people, Neruda sought to bring what had been happening (the past) directly into the actual (the present).

The historical event continues to be of significance only when it is remembered. However, the memory fades if there are no reminders. If my Uncle Al had never heard Neruda's poem read, perhaps he would never have examined his memories of Luis Muñoz Marín.

The pain was strong. I had learned to love and trust my family. Now I was reevaluating their information. I had to reach them. And the crisis was major. I had grown to trust all that my parents trusted, but now I could not. I began to learn about how their "facts" were given to them. I discovered that the bulk of the campaign propaganda of El Partido Popular, as led by Mr. Muñoz Marín, was commonplace cosmetic, industrial, democratic deceptions. I learned to cope with Mr. Muñoz Marín's lies, but I could not so easily get over understanding that my parents had been without political or economic insight and that all of the values of my childhood were false. My parents were victims of distorted, selected information. Nevertheless, their values were false and they did not awaken to the fact that it was up to them to confront the historical events of their lives.

Neruda makes you deal with the events of a past that is yours. History is personalized. It is attached to the individual. History, made concrete and contemporary, nourishes the memory of the individual and of the whole nation. It is a passionate process, and the tensions are intense. A well-told tale of forgotten tyrannies can revolutionize feelings and straighten out the lies of the past.

Luis Muñoz Marín was a public ruler, and around every public ruler, there is always a historical accounting of the events that took place. However, when a ruler grasps all forms of communications (newspapers, radio, TV) and destroys all objective accounting of events, someone must confront his historical account and present another. Neruda assigned himself that task in *Song of Protest*.

It was his intention to create unsettling and, whenever he felt it necessary, incendiary imagery:

> and his palace was white outside
> and inside it was infernal like Chicago
> with the mustache, the heart, the claws
> of that traitor, of Luis Muñoz the worm,
> Muñoz Marín to the people,
> Judas of the blood-let land,
> overseer of the enslavement of the island,
> corrupter of his poor brothers,
> bilingual translator for the executioners,
> chauffeur of North American whiskey.
>
> ("Muñoz Marín," II)

The chemistry of this passage can change learned habits. If you believe in Mr. Muñoz Marín, it arrests you because it makes you angry and it also precipitates you into violent confrontation with the poet. The poet engages himself to an extreme, and the reader has no choice but to respond in the extreme as well. It is a powerful device full of rich and painful consequences.

As I acquired information, I tried to bring it home to my family. But my consciousness was not complete. I became angry at the fact that my parents had not known. My Uncle Al must have felt my intentional insult to him as I read Neruda's poem. Instead of using the poem as a vehicle of illumination, I used it as a weapon of offense, an accusation:

> meanwhile Muñoz of Puerto Rico
> falsifies his island's signature
> and under the pirate's banner
> he sells out language and reason, lands, and delight,
> sells our poor America's honor,
> sells parents and grandparents and ashes.
>
> ("It Is Happening," III)

When there is no distance between the past and the present, the moment is thick with a sense of immediacy. It is like standing on the street and catching out of the corner of the eye a man who mugged you two months ago. Many intentions flood the mind. Revenge. Rush him. Cool it. He's armed. Call a cop. Push him in front of the First Avenue bus. Approach him and talk him into penitence. Run away. Call for help. It goes on and on until he is out of sight and the past and the present are not in perfect conjunction. Your mind reviews the shoving, the pushing, and the fear that his cold steel blade aroused in your heart, but by the time you reach Second Avenue, the present is going rampant and the past fades out of sight though it still evokes fear.

Neruda's poems have the power to jolt the memory in exactly the same way that it is jolted by the man who robbed you. The poems bring you Neruda's images as an offering of love; the thief came and took, Neruda comes and gives, but his gift is not one of mild fragrances from the east or west. It is a gift armed to give you a memory. In "Ancient History," he leaves Puerto Rico and moves onto Cuba, where he describes an island full of wholesome natural beauty. Here is an image of what was:

> Now I open my eyes, and I remember:
> it sparkles and dims, electric and dark,
> with joys and suffering
> the bitter and magic history of Cuba.
> Years passed as fish pass
> through the blue of the sea and its sweetness,
> the island lived in liberty and dance,
> the palm trees danced with the foam,
> Blacks and Whites were a single loaf of bread
> because Martí kneaded their ferment,
> peace fulfilled its destiny of gold,
> and the sun crackled in the sugar,
> while ripened by the sun fell
> a beam of honey over the fruit:
> man was content with his reign
> and the family with its agriculture . . .
>
> ("Ancient History," VI)

It was not a perfect past. But among its imperfections, there lived an image maker, José Martí, and his words had changed racial hatred and had blended mutinous wills into one. However, the local beauty "ripened by the sun" was soon to be raped:

> when from the North arrived a seed
> threatening, covetous, unjust,
> that like a spider spread her threads
> extending a metallic structure
> that drove bloodied nails into the land
> raising over the dead a vault.
> It was the dollar with its yellow teeth,
> commandant of blood and grave.
>
> ("Ancient History," VI)

Martí saw the betrayal and moved against a "dollar" morality in Cuba. He faced a violent foe. It was "hard and dark work / to lift an independent laurel: / to dream of liberty was danger." (IX) Neruda wrote about men who worked out with the problems of the present. Men who confronted destructive authority gave Neruda hope, and for these men he wrote songs that celebrated their deeds because he saw their courage:

> but Martí with hope and gunfire
> awakened the daydreamer and the peasant
> building with blood and thought
> the architecture of the new light.
>
> ("I Remember a Man," IX)

But their courage was always betrayed.

The betrayal was possible from any direction. In Nicaragua, Augusto C. Sandino "unloaded his sacred gunpowder / against assaulting sailors / grown and paid for in New York." (X) His struggle brought hope, but it was never suspected that he could win, that he could stop a foe that "dressed" so well for war:

> the Yankee did not expect what was happening:
> he dressed very well for war
> shining shoes and weapons.
>
> ("That Friend," X)

Sandino's guerrillas "came forth / even from the whiskey that was opened." It was a bloody confrontation which Sandino won. "That Friend" is a powerful poem that evokes the daring of great fighters. The West Point fighters came armed with "learned" tactics. They had no field experience. They had new technological weapons and expensive uniforms but no experience and no understanding of the passion that inspired Sandino and his men to fight:

> the North Americans did not learn
> that we love our sad beloved land
> and that we will defend the flags
> that with pain and love were created.
> If they did not learn this in Philadelphia,
> they found it out through blood in Nicaragua:
> the captain of the people waited there:
> Augusto C. Sandino he was called.
>
> ("That Friend," X)

Neruda told it so that the historical account could be cleared. He wanted the world to know that there were men who felt capable of confronting and defeating the rule of the dollar.

But the tyrant against independent Latin American governments was powerful, rich and very deceptive:

> For peace, on a sad night
> General Sandino was invited
> to dine, to celebrate his courage,
> with the 'American' Ambassador
> (for the name of the whole continent
> the pirates have usurped.)
> General Sandino was joyous:
> wine and drinks raised to his health:
> the Yankees were returning to their land
> desolately defeated,
> and the banquet sealed with honors
> the struggle of Sandino and his brothers.
> The assassin waited at the table.
> He was a mysterious, spineless being
> raising his cup time and again

while in his pocket resounded
the thirty horrendous dollars of the crime.

("Treason," XI)

Sandino was only one of the many fighting rulers who had been assassinated as they strove to govern without interference:

Sandino stood up not knowing
that his victory had ended
as the Ambassador pointed him out,
thus fulfilling his part of the pact:
everything was arranged for the crime
between the assassin and the North American.
And at the door as they embraced him,
they bade him farewell, condemning him.
Congratulations! And Sandino took his leave
walking with the executioner and death.

("Death," XII)

The work of one man can be stopped only if his action is not rooted in a public movement. Sandino's work was interrupted but not stopped. However, Nicaragua saw a powerful and long-lasting dictatorship assume power:

The killer of Sandino belonged to the "guardia nacional," a constabulary created by the United States to keep order after the marines had left. The leader of this force was a tough little warrior named Anastasio Somoza but familiarly called "Tacho." Somoza was also the nephew of President Sacasa, during whose administrations he acquired a strong grip on the mechanisms of power. Soon, he was announcing his advent to the presidency, implying that no one had better try to stop him. No one did. Somoza was the sole candidate in 1936, and he remained in power until he was assassinated twenty years later.

(John Edwin Fagg, Latin America, A General History,
New York, 1969. "The Traitor Dies," XIII.)

Somoza's assassination did not eliminate his influence from government. On the contrary, it was as if when Rigoberto Lopez killed Somoza, a plague had been released over all of Nicaragua:

> But from the guts that spilled
> came little Somozas:
> two clowns splattered with blood:
> from the cruel frog two little fertile frogs.
> Scarcely had the purulent one decayed,
> the two toy generals ascended,
> they embroidered themselves with diamonds;
> became lifetime presidents
> Dividing all of the haciendas between themselves
> they posed as *nouveaux riches*
> making themselves the favorite warriors
> of the North American Ambassador.
> That is how history is made in our land:
> thus crimes are perpetuated:
> and the chain of the infamous persists
> in a cesspool of military tortures.
>
> ("Monarchs," XIV)

This tale of United States intervention in the national affairs of Latin American nations holds for the whole of the continent. It is a story full of violent aggression and deceptions. Neruda relates how he "saw the rose [of resistance] bloom in Guatemala," but that Guatemala "was assassinated / in full flight, like a dove" ("In Guatemala," XVI). He also depicts the brutal spilling of blood in El Salvador, where "a bloody flavor soaks / the land, the bread and wine" ("In Salvador, Death," XVII).

When brought into the present the past arouses feelings of anger if what is being portrayed is a tale of tyranny and humiliation. It is clear to me that a Venezuelan reading the historical account that Neruda presents in poems XXIII to XXVI would find himself aroused to a pitch of anxiety. The events are so boldly stated and so passionately portrayed that I can see how a young Venezuelan reading a poem like "The Tiger" to his family might encounter the same crisis that I found myself in when I first read "Muñoz Marín" to my Uncle Al:

> Gómez was the name of that death.
> In half an hour he auctioned the petroleum
> to delinquent North Americans . . .
> fervent Venezuela bled.
> Gabaldón told me how from his cell
> he heard his comrade cry,
> he did not know what was happening
> until those short, cruel screams
> ended. And that was Venezuela's
> silence: no one answered.
> The worms and death lived.
>
> ("The Tiger," XXIV)

It is Neruda's personal contact with the history of Latin America that matters here. His involvement in the action is what makes him a purifier of the distorted historical record. To have a clear historical perspective, the poet had had to be in touch with the men who risked their lives. It is because of Neruda's direct involvement that the poems are such powerful indictments against the events that unfurled:

> but Pérez Jiménez buried
> Venezuela and tormented her.
> Her stores were filled with pain,
> torn limbs and broken bones
> and the prisons once again were
> populated with the most honest men.
>
> ("Pérez Jiménez," XXV)

Honest men in jail. Thieves on the streets adorning themselves with the public's trust. Yet even when armed insurrection managed to topple these treacherous leaders, even when "the walls of the tyrant were broken / and the people unfettered their majesty," these defeated rulers found a "palace" in the "Free World" which awaited them with open arms.

Neruda perceived with clarity that the ruling class of Latin Americans was inexorably subservient to foreign interests. Rómulo Betancourt, Neruda informs us, was first an opportunist with foreign economic allegiances, and then secondly the President of Venezuela:

> Recommended by Muñoz Marín,
> at last they certified him in New York
> with titles of specialist in law and order,
> the gringos studied him a moment
> and deposited him in Caracas,
> wrapped up in their perspective:
> he learned English in order to obey orders,
> he was prompt and circumspect in everything:
> eyes and ears toward North America
> while to Venezuela deaf and blind.
>
> ("A Strange Democrat," XXVI)

Information about the past without an active memory to bring historical details into the present is static information that does not service people. Neruda understood that it is one of the primary responsibilities of the poet to be the living, accurate memory of his people.

II. IMMEDIACY

When I am told a lie that is believed by the people I live with but not by me, I am alone. I remember sitting in a barbershop when the news of President Kennedy's death came over the radio. The President of the United States had been shot, and it was only a matter of hours before the media was flooded with assurances to the public that there had been no conspiracy, that it was the act of only one man: one solitary force carrying out its will without a "plot." I saw that the public wanted to believe that there had been no larger context for Oswald's action other than his own "nuttiness." I then saw the televised assassination of Lee Harvey Oswald. It, too, was believed to be the act of a solitary will doing its own most powerful bidding. Jack Ruby shortly thereafter died of cancer. No context. No conspiracy. Just individual men doing their thing. I did not believe it. But the people I loved and trusted believed it, and that made me feel frustrated and anxious.

What do I do when I am told a lie about events that have happened in my lifetime? I listen for stories. I do not enter disputes on President Kennedy's murder. I do what Neruda taught me to do. I just let information cruise in from wherever it is coming, and I then work at making a memory of the stories that are clear to me. Fidel Castro is a clear story; thus Neruda believed and celebrated Castro's work:

> But when torture and darkness
> seem to extinguish the free air
> and it is not the spume of the waves
> but the blood among the reefs that you see,
> Fidel's hand comes forth and in it
> Cuba, the pure rose of the Caribbean.
> And so History teaches with her light
> that man can change that which exists
> and if he takes purity into battle
> in his honor blooms a noble spring.
>
> ("Cuba Appears," IV)

The "tortures" are the lies, the distortion of events. The "darkness" is the fear that is experienced when there is no clarity, no story to believe. There are men who can deal with such times because they "can change that which exists." Neruda saw in Fidel Castro the "purity" of a self that put into action what he saw had to be done:

> Fidel Castro with fifteen of his men,
> and liberty touched down on the sand.
>
> ("The Challenge," V)

It was a simple and humble beginning. Fidel Castro began to create his Cuba with a "handful of men on the sand."

The war waged on Fidel Castro (once it was clear that he was going to retain his right to rule independent of the dollar) is just now becoming current "news" in the serious journals of our nation. The story as told by Taylor Branch and George Crile III in *Harper's* is a story that lays out events that were up to now thought of only as the nightmare dreams of schizophrenic left-wing propagandists and revolutionaries:

> During the last days of the Eisenhower Administration, the assassination of Fidel Castro presented itself as an engaging possibility to various people in Washington who had reason to mistrust a successful revolution so close to the coast of Florida. Some of these people discussed the possibility with the CIA, which had arranged sudden changes of government in Guatemala and Iran, and it has been said that a few agents left for the Caribbean with instructions to bring about a coup d' etat. Little more was heard from them until the debacle at the Bay of Pigs.
> (Editors' Introduction to Taylor Branch and George Crile III, "The Kennedy Vendetta: How the CIA waged a silent war against Cuba," *Harper's*, August, 1975.)

Neruda knew who Eisenhower was, and he made it plain to the world that Eisenhower's duplicity was a bitter cruelty:

> My theme is about a ship that came
> filled with ammunition and happiness:
> its cargo exploded in La Habana,
> its agony was an ocean on fire.
> There were two Eisenhowers in partnership,
> one navigated under water,
> and the other smiled in Argentina;
> one deposited the explosive,
> the other knighted the approaching men;
> one pushed the torpedo button,
> the other lied to all America,
> one swam like a green octopus,
> and the other was milder than an aunt.
> ("The Explosion of 'La Coubre' 1960," XXXI)

The problem of dealing with the immediate present is that accurate information about it is often not what the public believes.

The crisis occurs when I cannot believe public information and I am left with feelings of loneliness and wrongdoing. That is why I look for people to believe with me what the majority of people do not. It is an isolated position that makes me vulnerable because it makes me fear. I live aware that there is no "safety," and that the environment I exist in is in crisis. Neruda insists on pointing out the crisis because it is the antidote to sleep. It never matters how deep the sleep has been. What matters is the awakening of consciousness as the individual deals with what is happening.

Neruda saw Castro as the antidote to Cuba's sleep. He perceived the deliberate web of lies that was spun around Castro as he worked to put his words into action:

> Fidel, Fidel, the people are grateful
> for words in action and deeds that sing.
>
> ("To Fidel Castro," XIX)

"Words in action" is the key to Neruda's perception. A man who carries out his word is a man who makes himself concrete. Fidel was doing in Cuba what he "said" he would do, and that was surprising to those who thought that they could engage his services once he acquired power. The test of wills was on. Fidel Castro was confronted by the fears of weak Latin American leaders and President Kennedy's personal humiliation over the disaster of the Bay of Pigs:

> In Washington, President Kennedy struggled to comprehend how so total a disaster could have been produced by so many people who were supposed to know what they were doing, who had wrecked governments other than Castro's without mishap or detection. They had promised him a secret success but delivered a public fiasco. Communist rule in Cuba was to have been overthrown and Fidel Castro executed by Cuban citizens, all without evidence of American involvement; instead, Castro was heaping scorn on the "imperialist worms" he had defeated. Not only was the invasion an abject military failure, but the

highest officials of the U. S. government were being subjected to worldwide ridicule for having tried to pass it off as the work of independent Cubans. The CIA's elaborate "cover story" had fallen into absurdity, and the President finally ended the charade by issuing a statement in which he assumed full responsibility for the invasion. With this admission, the Bay of Pigs became a virtual synonym for international humiliation, as well as the most egregious display of official American lying yet entered into the public record.

(Branch and Crile, op. cit.)

Inside the United States, the crisis "let loose the fear of war and rallied public opinion to the President's support." I did not rally around our President. But many friends of mine, including members of my family, began to deride Castro as an enemy. I saw the public animosity that grew as our media and statesmen came out against Castro. Neruda met their assertions with his story:

> It seems that nowadays
> lies gather against Cuba
> the wire dispatches them day and night
> preparing for the moment of attack:
> "It seems that the church is distrustful"
> "There is discontent in Cayo Benito"
> "Fidel did not show on the 28th"
>
> ("The Ambush," XXI)

Neruda saw the "ambush" that awaited Castro and he also saw how Castro survived the lies while:

> meeting with other "latinos"
> equally sold out and perverse
> who yarn the lies of hell
> against Cuba each day:
> they alone concoct this stew.
>
> ("The Ambush," XXI)

It is now public knowledge that costly plots and military action against Castro were paid for and run by CIA agents. Yet Castro survived the rich and international power of the CIA. This is a deed that no other Latin American revolutionary leader has accomplished. Fidel Castro has weathered the severest storm of technological sabotage and espionage waged by the CIA in the Caribbean. Castro's crisis and the war that he is winning against the CIA have made clear to the world that with determination a rich enemy can be stopped and his lies exposed. Our present investigations of CIA covert activities inside our national borders testify to the tyrannous power that this agency has acquired.

But as Castro carries out his word and people come to believe in how he works, a collective story in which to believe will grow in Cuba. In the immediate present, however, Castro faces the crisis of having to deal with the confusion of deliberately spun lies and attacks against Cuba that are financed by millions of dollars on an international scale by the CIA. Neruda had seen what was happening. He also knew that Castro would need a troubadour, a man who would sing the deeds that he performed. Neruda assigned himself the task of being that storyteller:

> I was born to sing these sorrows
> to expose destructive beasts . . .
> I stir up the grief of my people,
> I incite the root of their swords,
> I caress the memory of their heroes,
> I water their subterranean hopes,
> for to what purpose my songs,
> the natural gift of beauty and words,
> if it does not serve my people
> to struggle and walk with me?
>
> ("I Come from the South," XV)

III. ACTION

Neruda took his information right out of his experience, and he got his energy replenished by being with people:

> I am the man of bread and fish,
> and you will not find me among books,
> but with women and men:
> they have taught me the infinite.
>
> ("So Is My Life," XXII)

People are the subject matter of these poems. The intention of the book is to "attend to the pain / of those who suffer: they are my pains" (XXII). Neruda sees it as his duty to assign himself the task of recorder. No outside force could have made him write these poems. It is an internal need to inform what is at work. Neruda set out to create a "historical flow" that would counter the "official" ignorance in which street people are kept:

> Some people ask me that human affairs
> with names, surnames and laments
> not be dealt with in the pages of my books,
> not to give them space in my verses:
> they say poetry died here;
> some say I should not do it:
> the truth is I do not want to please them.
>
> ("Do Not Ask Me," XXIX)

Assigning the self a task to carry out is an effort toward balance and a grasp at sanity. When Neruda can believe in nothing, he gives himself something to do and he then labors to make it through his self-assigned task:

> And so, if when I attack what I hate,
> or when I sing to those I love,
> poetry wants to abandon
> the hopes of my manifesto,
> I'll follow the letter of my law . . .
>
> ("Do Not Ask Me," XXIX)

The "letter" of Neruda's law is to move the potential power of the memory into action. Neruda works to bring the past into the now so that people can pay attention to the place that they are inhabiting:

> If you did not see the crimson of the "corocoro"
> flying like a suspended hive
> cutting the air like a scythe,
> the whole sky beating in flight
> as the scarlet plumage passes
> leaving a burning lightning bolt,
> if you did not see the Caribbean air
> flowing with blood without being wounded,
> you do not know the beauty of this world;
> you are not aware of the world you've lived in.
>
> ("Caribbean Birds," XXVII)

The poet pays attention to the immediate environment, to the geography of the nation, to the beauty of the land. Neruda creates powerful images in order to bring geographical sight to people:

> Panama, your geography granted you
> a gift that no other land was given:
> two oceans pushed forward to meet you:
> the cordillera tapered naturally:
> instead of one ocean, it gave you the water
> of the two sovereigns of the foam;
> the Atlantic kisses you with lips
> that habitually kiss the grapes,
> while the Pacific Ocean shakes
> in your honor its cyclonic stature.
>
> ("History of a Canal," XXXIII)

Neruda balances his beautiful geographical descriptions with an equally accurate reminder of the economic crime that is being committed against the land:

> but men from other parts
> brought to you their yoke
> and they spilled nothing but whiskey
> since they mortgaged your waistline:
> and everything follows as it was planned
> by devils and their lies:
> with their money, they built the Canal;
> they dug the earth with your blood

and now dollars are sent to New York,
leaving you the graves.

("History of a Canal," XXXIII)

Neruda's perception tuned itself into the crisis of the moment. His task was to create images that would make the moment so rich with memories that he and people along with him would flow into action.

Many of the poems in *Song of Protest* create geographical images that describe and celebrate the natural beauty of the continent. Neruda was seeking a balance between giving people a memory and describing for them the natural riches that they actually live in. Both faculties are needed to have a grasp of what is happening. A man needs a memory and a live relationship with the land in order to develop independent muscles:

like Panamanian wind asks
like a child that has lost its mother
where is the flag of my country?

("History of a Canal," XXXIII)

Neruda inspires personal action. The poems do not present a theory or a plan toward a revolution. Instead, Neruda creates historical and geographical pictures that stimulate the mind of the reader into the real. His action is to deliver a geographical-historical charge into his reader's muscle. In "The Heroes," Neruda swiftly sketches the fate of the men and women who have risked putting their muscles into action:

But the students who shoot
against evil, alone or scattered,
will find no asylum in Embassies;
nor will they find ships in port;
nor planes to transport them to another place,
unless it's to where torments await them.
They will be denied a visa to New York
until the young clandestine hero
is, later, denounced and discovered:

they will leave no eyes in sockets,
one by one, they will crush the bones.
Later, they will show off at the UN
in this Free World of ours,
while the North American Minister
gives Trujillo new weapons.
This tale is terrible, and if you have suffered,
you will forgive me, I do not lament it.
That is how the wicked perpetuate themselves:
this is reality and I do not lie.

("The Heroes," XXXVIII)

War is not the only road to a balance, and Neruda makes it clear in "North American Friend" that he can see that there is hope for mutual understanding with the northern "workers broad, narrow and bent / over wheels and flames." Neruda does not visualize the north as only a place full of monsters and liars. He asserts that he wants to share learning, but he finds that:

. . . Two or three people
close the North American doors
and only the "Voice of America" is heard,
which is like listening to a lean chicken.

("North American Friend," XXXIX)

In the United States, we ourselves have been satiated with "listening" to the "lean chicken" broadcasts that carry the lies of our national government around the world. We have just been discovering the need to expose the deceptions that the highest officers of our land release to us through an incessant media that carries public announcements of falsehood into the most private spaces of our lives. The media could be a positive instrument for shaping future time, but for now it pecks at our lives with its endless attacks on our senses as it sells us merchandise that in the getting depletes the world's natural resources. Neruda sees through to this nation's greed when he speaks his balanced vision:

We are not going to exploit your petroleum;
we will not intervene with customs,

we will not sell electrical energy
to North American villages:
we are peaceful people who can
be content with the little we earn
we do not want to submit anyone
to coveting the circumstances of others.
We respect Lincoln's space
and Paul Robeson's clear conscience.
We learned to love Charlie Chaplin
(although his power was evilly rewarded).
And so many things, the geography
that unites us in the desired and,
everything tells me to say once again
that we are sailing in the same boat:
it could sink with pride:
let us load it with bread and apples,
let us load it with Blacks and Whites,
with understanding and hopes.

("North American Friend," XXXIX)

Neruda proposes a vision of unity that we have not yet achieved inside the national borders of the United States. We are not going to find unity with Latin America either until we settle the domestic problem of public lies told us in the name of "National Security." Neruda does not conceive a need to come north to destroy or to be revenged. He simply teaches the expulsion of the dollar and the moral and economic manipulation that it imposes wherever it flourishes.

Neruda's final gesture in *Song of Protest* is to sing a song of praise. He sings the praise of the Sierra Maestra, whose rugged landscape had long offered a home to Cuban patriots. Neruda celebrates "the rough groves, / the tough habitat of the rocks" because he knew the risk that Castro was taking as he made himself a coherent story for the Cuban people to believe in. Castro's remarkable administration "had not lost its puritanical character, and it was probably the least corrupt that Cuba had known for decades." (John Edwin Fagg, *Latin America, A General History* [New York,

1969], p. 580.) Neruda felt deep trust in the purity of Castro's intention. He saw in Fidel a warrior who had the fire to purify the present and to create a future where clarity would prevail:

> I see what's coming and what's being born,
> the pains that were defeated,
> the destitute hopes of my people:
> the children in school with shoes,
> the giving out of bread and justice
> as the sun gives out with summer
> I see fulfilled simplicity . . .
>
> ("Written in the Year 2000," XLII)

In his meditation over the Sierra Maestra, Neruda projects his vision into future time as he perceives a world of working men where "there is no necessity to run / between governors and courts of justice" because it is a world in which "the cruel and the bad are gone forever." "Written in the Year 2000" is Neruda's vantage point from which he asserts:

> In this space the turbulent weight
> of my life neither overcomes nor weeps,
> I discharge the pain that visits me
> As I release a pigeon:
> if there is accounting to be done, it must be done
> with what's to come and what's beginning,
> with the happiness of all the world
> and not with what time crumbles
>
> ("Written in the Year 2000," XLII)

His meditation points the way to the joy of work. Each man delights in "what's to come" if he is the maker of it. Neruda asks that we look at "what's beginning." He shows that the action of one man never ends because "another takes mysterious arms: / human rebirth has no end . . . " In the last poem of *Song of Protest* (XLIII), Neruda announces a "Final Judgment" that he did not write because men of action are now just acquiring their independent muscles. Neruda leaves their fate on the heights of the Sierra Maestra to grow strong in their battle:

> I leave it on this summit protected,
> high, undulating over the prairies,
> representing for the oppressed peoples
> the dignity born out of fighting . . .
>
> ("Written in the Year 2000," XLII)

A Mongo Affair
(1975)

On the corner by the plaza
in front of
the entrance to González-Padín
in old San Juan,
a black Puerto Rican talks
about "the race"
he talks of Boricuas
who are in New York on welfare
and on lines waiting for food stamps,
"yes, it's true, they've been taken out
and sent abroad, and those that
went over tell me that they're
doing better over there than here;
they tell me they get money
and medical aid
that their rent is paid
that their clothes get bought
that their teeth get fixed
is that true?"
on the corner by the entrance to González- Padín
I have to admit that he has been
lied to, misled,
that I know that all the goodies
he named humiliate the receiver,
that a man is demoralized
when his woman and children
beg for weekly checks,
that even the fucking a man does
on a government bought mattress

draws the blood from his cock,
cockless, sin espina dorsal,
mongo—that's it!
a welfare fuck is a mongo affair!
mongo means flojo
mongo means bloodless
mongo means soft
mongo cannot penetrate
mongo can only tease,
but it can't tickle
the juice of the earth-vagina
mongo es el bicho Taíno
porque murió
mongo es el borinqueño
who's been moved
to the inner-city jungles
of north american cities,
mongo is the rican who survives
in the tar jungle of Chicago
who cleans, weeps, crawls,
gets ripped off,
sucks the eighty dollars a week
from the syphilitic
down deep frustrated
northern man—
viejo negro africano,
Africa Puerto Rico,
sitting on department store entrances
don't believe the deadly game
of northern cities paved with gold and plenty,
don't believe the fetching dream
of life improvement in New York
the only thing you'll find in Boston
is a soft leather shoe up your ass,
viejo, anciano africano, Washington
will send you in your old age

to clean the battlefields
in Korea and Vietnam;
you'll be carrying a sack,
and into that canvas
you'll pitch las uñas
los intestinos
las piernas
los bichos mongos
of Puerto Rican soldiers
put at the front to face
¡sí!
to face the bullets, bombs, missiles,
¡sí! the artillery
¡sí!
to face the violent hatred of Nazi Germany
to confront the hungry anger of the world,
viejo negro,
viejo puertorriqueño
the north offers us pain
and everlasting humiliation,
IT DOES NOT COUGH UP
THE EASY LIFE: THAT IS A LIE,
viejo que has visto la isla
perder sus hijos
are there guns to deal with
genocide, expatriation?
are there arms to hold
the exodus of borinqueños
from Borinquen?
we have been moved
we have been shipped
we have been parcel posted
first by water, then by air
el correo has special prices

for the "low island element" to be
removed, then dumped
into the inner-city ghettos
viejo, viejo, viejo
we are the minority
here in Borinquen,
we, the Puerto Ricans,
the original men and women of this island,
are in the minority
I writhe with pain
I jump with anger
I know
I see
I am "la minoría de la isla,"
viejo, viejo anciano
do you hear me?
there are no more Puerto Ricans
in Borinquen
I am the minority everywhere
I am among the few in all societies
I belong to a tribe of nomads
that roam the world without
a place to call a home,
there is no place that is ALL MINE;
there is no place that I can
call mi casa,
I, yo, Miguel ¡Me oyes viejo!
I, yo, Miguel
el hijo de María Socorro y Miguel
is homeless, has been homeless,
will be homeless
in the to be
and the to come
Miguelito, Lucky, Bimbo

you like me have lost
your home,
and to the first idealist
I meet I'll say,
don't lie to me
don't fill me full of vain
disturbing love for an island
filled with Burger Kings,
for I know there are no cuchifritos
in Borinquen
I remember last night
viejito lindo
when your eyes fired me
with trust,
do you hear that?
with trust
and when you said
that you would stand by me
should any danger threaten
I halfway threw myself
into your arms to weep
mis gracias
I loved you
viejo negro
I would have slept
in your arms
I would have caressed
your curly gray hair
I wanted to touch
your wrinkled face
when your eyes fired me
with trust
viejo corazón puertorriqueño
your feelings cocinan

en mi sangre
el poder de realizarme
and when you whispered
your anger into my ears
when you spoke of
"nosotros los que estamos
preparados con las armas,"
it was talk of future
happiness
my ears had not till
that moment heard such
words of promise and of guts
in all of Puerto Rico,
old man with the golden chain
and the medallion with an indian
on your chest
I love you
I see in you
what has been
what is coming
and will be
and over your grave
I will write
HERE SLEEPS
A MAN
WHO SEES ALL OF
WHAT EXISTS
AND THAT WHICH WILL EXIST.

Biological
(1975)

Puerto Rican
children
have nothing to
say in school.
Pedro said the
other day "I've
got the D train
running up my
leg and the F train
in my crotch."
The teacher gave
him a demerit
and said "Sit
down." He sat and
peed all down
his pants. The
teacher sent him
to the principal
for incorrigible
behavior. Pedro
knew he had not
been understood.
Puerto Rican
children
have nothing to
say in school.

Tangiers
(1975)

Down to the Kasba with me,
Miky, Dadi and Lucky
down to the Kasba with us
right into the hollering poverty
of Tangiers where boys sell
themselves for little more than
a dollar's caress, where people
are hungry, go hungry and
will remain under attack
from stomach cramps
and muscle spasms caused
by rampant malnutrition
Tangiers yo ya to quiero
estoy enamorado d'être ici
dans le nord d'Afrique
dans la ville la plus belle
que j'avais jamais vue—Tangiers
I love the happy tyranny of being
attacked on all sides for my
american connection "les dollars,"
the green mercurochrome that heals
all the scabby wounds of pennilessness
and homelessness and hunger,
Tangiers, your children are les
plus beaux du monde and yet
they scurry down your gutter-alleys
bleeding hopelessness,

Tangiers, your bleeding children speak
three, four, five languages before
they're five years old—your streets
create maximum survival pressure
making your children's tongues
control alternate systems of speech
as they hustle the cracks of the streets
and the queens from the continent—
four spanish queens glide into
the Café Central like Columbus's
ships must have slid into the new
world: grace, poise, perfume, vaseline
and an uncontrollable gleam in their eyes
as the boys parade themselves—
the older queen exhibits a skin as
wrinkled as Lady Wishfort's cracked
and peeling face
the other orders mint tea with little sugar
as his eyes anxiously rape a twelve-
year-old crotch, the boy smiles, a ten dirham
bill is flashed and a new romance has just
been bought, the other two devour every
young box that comes into sight and the
boys parade as the ladies' anxious helmet
jones keep coming down
beautiful boys approach
beautiful boys go away
beautiful boys approach
beautiful boys go away
all are for sale
ten dirhams for this one
twenty dirhams for the other
Tangiers is Forty-Second Street
morality with an Orchard Street

sales pitch—un muchachito
tuerto approaches; he tries us
out in french, italian, german
then english
he hit the jackpot, our ears betray
us, he knows we've understood him
now comes the onrush,
the insistence, the pleading,
the assault, the guilt trip
tripping us up sending our
hands into our pockets searching
for a dirham to leave our consciousness
clean, to buy us freedom from
the boy's imploring hustle
we are hand-to-mouth Nuyoricans
suddenly made rich by greater poverty
than our own
but wait!
Tangiers, our inner-city jungles
match yours, and they are equally
poor, dirty, misunderstood, desperate
and we are struggling, hustling men
just like your boys
but we exist inside the belly of the
monster, we are the pistons that
move the roughage through Uncle
Sam's intestines, we keep the flow
of New York happening
we are its muscles
and its castor oil
we are its poets, its historians,
its dishwashers, its toilet cleaners,
and its revolutionaries:
a revolutionary is un marchand ambulant,

a revolutionary is a petit taxi
carrying truth as its fare,
a revolutionary breathes through his mouth
while all others breathe through their
nose and in his throat he separates
the oxygen from the waste before
air reaches his lungs—
le Café Central at the Petit Chico
stays open 24 hours a day
and once again Miky and I
are at the pure heart
        the vibrating pulse
of Tangiers—people are drawn
around the square
like moscas to flypaper,
coffee, mint tea, toast, butter and
jelly, no beer no alcohol no wine
only café crême, talk and endless
begging—many blind men
        many maimed men
        many starving cats
        and hungry young boys
as I drink café crême, talk and give
dirhams when I'm moved to share
my short change,
I am reminded of the
        stratégies de l'économie
of Europe and I'm struck by the fact
that:
        les "managers" sont les
        moteurs de l'économie,
        l'age des masses a besoin
        de propulseurs qui sachent faire
        mouvoir les gens et les
        choses. Et le verbe anglais
        "to manage" ne signifie au

fond rien d'autre. Toutefois,
l'activité que couvre ce vocable ne
provient pas d'Angleterre ou
d'Amérique, mais d'Allemagne
England gave its language
the U.S. invented abstract management
now Germany takes it to heart and creates
les écoles les plus importantes de
cadres dirigéants privée dans le monde,
Spinola resigns in Portugal
while Miky, Lucky and I are
ready to become the managing
directors of the streets of Tangiers—
our first down to the money for food
trip happens with Toni,
Toni is making his économie
balance on the sale of our 1968
Ford Transit Van, our home for
sale in Tangiers streets, our
papers are not in legal order,
our first buyer offers two hundred
fifty, no more and be happy
you've got an offer
we decide not to sell Margarita-Tanya;
we're hundreds of dollars
short of what we've planned,
but wouldn't sell for two-fifty
since I didn't like getting pinned
by a slickster from the streets
of Tangiers where the rich live
and the very poor are the indicators
whereby a man can know he's rich
well anyway,
Toni and his buddy poured fear

into the atmosphere because of our
irregular papers proving ownership
of la voiture, we listened with respect,
but we left before eating with him,
we began to move our bed and
all our blankets back into the van and as
we reassembled our little moving
fortress we realized we were back
into our womb, our internal place
of private control which keeps us
all responsible for our moving on
our own—

LA ÚNICA DIFERENCIA ENTRE
UN ÁRABE Y UN PUERTORRIQUEÑO
ES LA MANERA EN QUE SOPLA EL VIENTO

THE ONLY DIFFERENCE BETWEEN
AN ARAB AND A PUERTO RICAN
IS THE WAY IN WHICH THE WIND
BLOWS

Sunday, August 11, 1974

Sunday afternoon and it is one-thirty and all the churchgoing latinos have crossed themselves and are now going home to share in the peace of the day, pan y mantequilla, una taza de café and many sweet recollections of el rinconcito en Juncos, donde Carmencita, María y Malén jugaban y peleaban.

Sunday afternoon and it is one-thirty and all the churchgoing latinos fuse each other with love and the women dress so clean and pure and the children walk so straight and pure and the fathers look so proud and pure and everything so right and pure and even as I wake up to my nephew's voice coming through the window, there is pleasure in awakening. My mother and father and Grafton and Johnny come in, there is light in
their eyes,
there is pleasure in living,
there is no shame in being
full of love,
there is no shame in being
nude while my mother's
eyes look in at me,
looking at my nude body,
body that she made mixing her blood
with my father's,
and there's no rushing for clothes
just sweet openness in being
loved by my family.
Sunday afternoon and it is
one-thirty and all the church-
going latinos have crossed themselves,
and my body swings free.

San Juan / an arrest / Maguayo / a vision of Malo dancing
(1975)

The VW breaks down on
the highway, and we seek
a mechanic. We are given
directions, and what we're
finding out is that
"it's nice to live in fear"
fear of police, fear of being
caught masturbating, fear,
fear of being caught,
apprehended, tú entiendes?
fear of having to answer
the questions of the law.
We were on our way
to Cupey after having been
in San Juan
¡no!
¡espérate! it was the other
way around. We had just
arrived. Lucky saw a woman,
he felt he pitied her
but really it was a queso jones
that got us into a scrap
with the cops—we thought
that getting off the plane
would drop us into the lap
of "la familia," we thought
we'd find a noble feeling

that we'd be sure and secure
that there would be a madre
alma to kiss our New York
soot-filled bodies and soul
pero cuando el policía
asked "where's your license?"
I said hey I've come to see
Borinquen to love her shores
to spread my beauty here
my NUYORICAN being
my eagle knife caution
filled mind reads your neon
signs AQUÍ YOUR CRÉDITO ES GOOD
and I feel sad that in school,
we're forced to reach for standards
do you know what I mean?
standards like
      STANDARD ENGLISH
      STANDARD SPANISH
but meanwhile your neon
signs tell the real truth:
you are bilingual Puerto Rico
you are NUYORICAN on
your own home soil,
your schools scold me for illiteracy
while your Cuban/American bankers
sell me the island in spanglish
(SPANGLISH-NUYORICAN)
and that's the truth
of the dollar matter
the conscience of Borinquen
is a spanish/english
neon nightmare,
but really it is all about
getting caught and having

to admit my license has
expired—"you're under
arrest" pero señor Policía
I am on Borinquen, and my
license is a fault of law,
but I am clean so let
me go and I'll send you
a poem—"you're under
arrest" twenty-five dollars later and much
humiliation we called it a draw,
and I was free to go—but
Lucky it was, sure enough
lucky, wasn't it?
the cop's eyes burned holes
through your clothes
the cop x-rayed your soul
but you were quicker
than god before his creation,
how beautiful when you
dropped your sack and the
papers spilled over the
street and the grass was
in among the papers and
as you handed the cop your
sack, you pulled the
papers together keeping
our ganga out of sight
how smooth
how easy it was
to keep our secret
yet how fast
how cunning
you were
when you shifted
your eyes from street to sack

to street to yourself standing
holding our weed between
the pages of your poems
and how clear it was
that el policía's eyes
couldn't x-ray the poems,
he couldn't
defeat the POEMS
he couldn't discover
our innocent smoke secret,
smooth,
cunning,
fast,
deliberate,
inside the self
that's what the street
Nuyorican has to learn
for survival, and that's
what Lucky knows—
he knows salvation is from inside
the self—
Maguayo home of el
jíbaro Puertoriqueño your
conscience, the smell of your
smartness is molded, born,
grown, nourished in the streets
of New York: in the Bon Soir
I see the energies of our nation
pour its sweat juice as
peals of electronic sounds pour
over sweated bodies
I see brown women being
brown women to pussydom
desiring, inventing the
deep down liberation of

being woman and in love
with woman-Butch and
the Sun-Dance Chick—
Borinquen, your beautiful
brown women love each other
in the public eye of the Bon Soir
as Malo's sweat
bathes each male eye
with wonder that his beautiful
masculinity can contort itself
in telling the dance tale
of the city—
City of New York
Malo tells the story of your
factory slaving police
intimidated working class,
each step enacts the work-
aday sexual torture of the
slums and your beautiful
boys without Christian parents
to sustain them in false virtue,
Malo the tortured electronic
sound of black America
becomes apple-pie cheddar
cheese wisdom to my eyes—
I see you are high on moving
faster than sight
your right leg
curled up to your waist
as you spread both hands
and sprint off your left leg—
Malo, do you see?
that that's the position your
factory-slave forefathers
have held as they've worked

the machinery of the city—
spin into hysteria
dance the working class roots
of your muscles into telling
the humiliation of your people
through motion—dance
and torture the air, writhe
your body into despair,
into the joy of dancing
out our pain/your pain
as well:
Maguayo
campo campo terrestre
de Puerto Rico
your children speak an English-
Spanish mixed salad,
the vulgar language of
the spirit that is to be.
Maguayo gracias por Lucky
and muchas, muchas
gracias for letting me feel
the soil of this island without
the neon lights of
north american night-
mare dream of TVs in every
bathroom
Maguayo
gracias por las letrinas
that connect my shit to myself
without the sanitary mania that
now rules our lives
Maguayo
te quiero porque los aguacates
cuestan quince chavos
Maguayo, you were and are

the proof of our lost innocence,
of our impurity,
Maguayo, we hardly own you
we barely make you our own
maybe
maybe
when Malo dances on your soil,
your holy baptism will
make you ours
to own
to keep
to build on—
Maguayo
the mosquitoes have bred
on your soil
after two weeks of rain,
they rape my soft skin,
they invade my fluids,
they suck my pores
free of the blood that I am
to offer,
me comen vivo,
me deboran la sangre,
there's something capitalistic
about mosquitoes: they feed till
they almost burst full of blood
and then they go on to seek
new survival energy,
to draw more blood elsewhere.
Maguayo your jibaro,
your survival
is Nuyorican not Taino,
not black, not white
just Nuyorican—
I'll tell you something more

Borinquen
as I sat all ñangotao there
in Maguayo
as I let my intestines have free
flow and as my constipation
won I realized I was just as
afraid in Borinquen
as I am in New York
pero te quiero Maguayo
porque los aguacates
cuestan quince chavos
te amo por la simplicidad
que le ofreces
a uno who lives in
524 E. 6th St.
New York, New York
          10009
My first night in Maguayo
began in a VW and
ended in a bed sleeping
three: Dadi, Miky and myself,
we slept easy till the morning
heat sent a fever of itch
to be up at the beach getting sun,
sun for my psyche,
sun for my skin,
sun for my nourishment,
sun for my vision—
the water at Boquerón is bath-
tub warm,
it touches gently,
the waves at Boquerón are light
gentle invasions,
the water is gentle,
the water seduces,

the water accommodates
itself around my balls
around the whole of my body,
at Boquerón six kilometers from
Maguayo the sensual truth
is that the waves seduce,
the waves arouse,
the waves gently lick
my free swinging head
the gentle knocks erect me,
the gentle sea waves
ebb and flow around my body
the whole of the Caribbean Sea
moves to the rhythm of my
opening pores
unleashing centers of passion
that squeeze my sperm
up / through to the head,
the moves are quick
the sea is gentle
the breeze caresses
my spine jerks hard
my skin stretches
to the rhythm of the sea—
the sea's a ring around my rosie
and I am the father of the
oceans as my sperm
swims right up into
the world's wide open SEAS.

Happy New Year
January 1, 1976

Cold chills invade my body
and my electrical connections are perspiring
and it's short-circuit time,
pero coño maybe there's no time like short-circuit time.
Gil's been asking why there's not been more
poetry and I keep feeling that there's
poetry in the making all the time
it's just that I've got to keep translating it
into visual terms that mean something
to everybody else as cold chills invade my body
in the new year, why is it I learn
everything through pain? why, que pasa,
porqué is it that I'm always
running on icy sidewalks and pushing my
psychic program to destruction? So what if the
drinks are free at the Tin Palace,
I keep asking for soda and rum
flooding my body till it rebels,
turning around the peristaltic waves
as it rejects all of my fluids and food
and I lose my energies, become real
weak, dizzy, disruptive storm
immobilizes my faculties till I cannot hold together
in balance my muscles and my electrical energy,
the rebellion in my gut forcing me to rush
to the men's room to puke and drool into the
toilet, helplessly looking at myself in the mirror
as I involuntarily emit chicken noodle soup,
wine and rum and gasp for air in between
the rushes where the stomach gathers a new wave
of energy to spit out of my mouth,

I've tried to write while vomiting
but the sickness is messy and I end up
with a page splattered with yesterday's rice and beans
and veal cutlet parmigiana pickled in rum, wine and pot
cold chills invade my body
when Bimbo shows the anguish of his mind
and despairs that living on Avenue B between
6th & 7th streets keeps him delivering his child to
Bellevue's emergency room for lung treatment
because too much ghetto dirt has clogged his
lungs, cold chills invade his little body
while fever, coughing and general muscular pain
stunt his growth, Bimbo can't place his vision
above the conditions of his family,
        his cultural vision
has to put food on the family table
only then will his dream be healthy,
that's it, eso es,
        a man's vision
has to feed his life or
        else
his vision belongs to air and offers
no security at all leaving him and us out
in the cold, shielding ourselves with disappearing words
and castor oil dreams as Bimbo's disillusionment
climbs out looking around trying to purge itself,
        he is a hero this Bimbo
he places his blood pulse on the line that binds
his will to do all that he says he can do
and has done and will continue to do
        this hero, this intellectual giant
        from 6th St. esta encojonar
embrollado and trying to purge
his malady letting out the cancerous symptoms
that brew in men and the ambulatory visions
of their heads when money pinches inspiration
away leaving them hungry, coatless and homeless
cold chills invade their bodies and mine.

New Year's Eve
December 31, 1975

Richie playing the maracas
is the universe becoming fluid
and the Nuyorican Café
floor becoming platform
for the shape of art
to mimic so that the artifact
becomes direct message
　　no symbols of
　　but the very thing itself
the knife in the belly
and the blues singing soft
shoes of pain as my gut
kicks my nerves insisting
on its pain vomiting more pain
about gifts that on a Christmas
day reached a dead child
too late to be played with
but it wasn't the deliverer's fault
it was his uncle who kept forgetting
that Christmas falls with love
not on a calendar but on the tenderest
feelings where the self of all others wants
love and sharp edges that awake
the internal mind into a self-created speech
that reaches over into your listener's system
and reschedules his entire psychic set,
I once had a friend who in one afternoon

traced all of my spinal short-circuits
and rearranged my electrical flow
into more fluid work than the switch-on,
switch-off, I'm overloaded crisis
that results in nausea, asphyxiation and the
swallowing of my tongue
      hay algo
      hay un epileptic fit
trying to reduce me into a trembling
mass of jellied nerves, formless,
shuddering, there, on the subway floor
while hundreds of passengers masochistically
look on both enjoying my crisis and feeling sorry
for me, the poor wretch, lying on the dirty
concrete subway floor imploring my muscles
and nerves to keep cool and cut the short-
circuit tongue down my throat menace
out and institute a no-nonsense
coherent I'm a mechanical and predictable
human being behavior modification program
to counter my muscular violence against myself
which keeps calling attention to itself while the
transit cop is almost breaking both my legs
by throwing his full weight on me as he
tries to hold my legs still and my mouth open
grabbing at my tongue, yanking it out,
shaking my shoulders, slapping my face,
working to neutralize the short-circuit
in my spine till Dr. Psychiatrist starts
to define my mind and its connections
into a State Asylum where I can get more
medication than I do out on the streets
or have the medication forced on me by a
well-meaning nurse who relates herself to me

through an every four hour give him his
dosage routine
 hay algo
 it's 11:59 p.m. 1975
and I got one more minute of talk
before 1976 finds me shooting up and down
behind the Nuyorican Café bar trying to
decide if nuclear war will ravage
New York before I find out just how
to divide the line so that it repairs
short-circuits that block the world
from coming together! it is 12 a.m.
the new year's been bombed and over the T.V.
the hottest news release tells us that at La Guardia
Airport an explosion was so strong that tiny,
invisible slivers of glass have penetrated the skin
of many but the slivers are so fine that
it cannot be detected where they've entered
the body
and here it is 1976 enters in like a
glass sliver undetected yet causing pain.

Day after Christmas
December 26, 1975

Edwina playing the quinto
Stephanie playing the conga
Fanny playing the tumba
as a whirl of conga rhythms
melt the fat off of my
constipated mind and I feel,
there, all there, totally unsoiled,
being made, created by pure skin
around a steel rim pulsing
vibrations chock full of nutty
feelings that resonate the full of my
lips rounding my lady's womb
with my saliva warmth,
       oh I wish you a Merry Xmas
       and a happy New Year,
Edwina closes her eyes and beats
messages of pure feelings
into our ears and I run up
and down behind the bar
serving the wine and beer
that oil the inspiration of street
grown poets who talk to god
and god alone about their harsh
street survival,
       yo quiero sol,
I do not want to live in shade
and Stephanie and Fanny put light
in my eyes when I feel their rhythms

in light flashes that brighten
my darkest most tormented
nights as I pull these rhythms
out of my memories into
my present and send all
the shades away.

Christmas Eve: Nuyorican Café
December 24, 1975

Slow by slow people come
to celebrate the birth of
    jesus rodriguez,
John comes in releasing joyous vibes,
has a beer, gives me a rap about his
party in the Bronx and how he's coming
down with everybody later on to celebrate
Noche Buena at the café,
one more night of people searching to make
contact with each other and jesus is
the living pretext,
     jesus,
     jesus rodriguez
hoy es tu cumpleaños,
tonight on the eve of your birth
I sit weaving electrical impulses
with Willy One, Ruben and the talking
coconut, el Señor Jorge Brandon, who
bears the flag of poetry on his tongue
and purest love in his heart giving it
away on the impulse of the moment,
generously to anybody ready to control
the ego and become a listener to a master
painter with words, today jesus rodriguez
was born, and el gran poeta Brandon
brings words that change
the listener as he tells in word paintings

the pain of falling in love with woman
and the disaster that jealousy
initiates when man and woman
do not trust each other,
    but here it is and it is
    Christmas day and today
    jesus rodriguez is born
and men and women will cease
to be jealous, and green will only
mean spring, rejuvenation,
    not evil
    disintegrating
    jealousy,
jesus is born speaking Nuyorican
eating tortillas con salchichas
to the rhythms of winter hot
conga drums that
    lament an ice cold Christmas
    that slips away under a slight
    blanket of Christmas snow.

A Sixty-One-Year-Old Junkie
(1978)

We knew where we were
and we knew what we had to do,
we had come to see Willy B
but we had forgotten his phone
and he didn't have a bell
"yoh, Willy B," Miky yelled,
Lucky whistled, and I stood
looking up hoping to rouse him
"yoh, Willy B," Lucky yelled,
Miky whistled and I stood
looking up hoping to rouse
Willy B from his apomorphine
non-addictive normalcy,
"Willy B," we three shouted,
"Willy B," rouse yourself,
come out of your morphine
bathed in hydrochloric acid
balance and open the door
cause we want you to sew
Miky's guts back into his belly,
they were torn out last night
when a street surgeon smarting
from a beat came to operate
so that he could regain his
emasculated pride, "yoh, Willy B,"
Miky's bleeding to death
and Lucky's falling asleep

and I'm losing my flesh
as the night air melts it away,
"yoh, Willy B. open up!"
Slow by slow Willy B came
down the stairs, opened the door
and looked into the night air
finding six eyes all straight
and bared of the illusions of the
crib where mother-protection
had fooled us into trusting everywhere,
"Willy B, I'm Miguel and
this is Lucky and Miky."
"Please come in, I'm upstairs,"
said Willy B, gesturing us to enter
and climb the stairs
thus breaking up our long stare
into his vodka-eyes glare,
we climbed
into the inner-vein-womb
of a Lower Soho sixty-one-
year-old junkie's writing haven,
Willy B's ice eyes of eyes that are my eyes
of ice, I looked at the ice-age
glare of Willy B and felt at home
in their frigid loneliness,
I smelled the sex of his respiration
but I heard the impotence of his touch
of flesh,
Willy B, you macho masochist
from Tangiers spreading spiritual
apomorphine breath while desiring more
speedball visions, do you smell
your allegedly unwashed feet
          "Willy B,"

you're a tall tale teller of
mythic lies about yourself, but
then again I am a liar of self as well,
the difference being that my Nuyorican
lies are concrete spun and yours
the junkie tales of calloused veins
in Tangiers wonderland where Arab
boys run out towards freedom selling
miraculous sex,
     "Willy B"
I know you've felt the universe
     "yoh, Willy B"
dickery, dickery dick
where is my kicky dick,
I think I've dicked
the darkest hole of our palmolive
revlon red rouged raped universe
     "yoh, Willy dick,
      Oh, tricky dick"
rouse my un-heroined capitalistic
synapses into a socialism of the
soul where everybody shits into
everybody else's mouth so that we
can destroy all ego,
all sense of Yo or I,
the I that is not yet invisible
make me invisible
and not perchance to dream
of being visible
but truly invisible
beyond the leprosy of melting flesh
and being tiger in a dried lamb's coat
sharing a beer with a sixty-one-year-
old junkie in his Lower Soho loft

without personality,
why I almost kissed your shadow
when you handed me a glass of beer
held by your fingers shaking in their
vodka-rage,
          "yoh, Willy B"
I videotaped my flick with Anais late last
night and played it back while I fucked
her in the ass and found that I'm a
monster when I pack a woman's shit
driving my love and anger loco style
right into the schizophrenia of her
lower colon, feeling her inner womb
with four fingers stretched to touch
the warmth where children get born
and pussies get torn,
          "yoh, Willy B,"
Slow by slow Willy B and we came
down the stairs, opened the door
and he let us out into the night air.

Allegro Brillante
(1978)

On the Nuyorican Poets' Café floor,
Eddie on the timbales,
Freddie, just walked in, on the quinto,
John on the conga,
Luz playing maracas,
Max on the trumpet
Carlos on electric guitar
and T.C. repeating "suave, suave,"
        take your time,
        time,
        take your
        time,
        your time take,
        fast is slow,
        show is fast,
your time take for yourself,
for yourself take your time,
speed up and slow tip
according to the tempo of your
inner rhyme scheme,
the jiggling flow of feeling
that unites me to the stern of the rose
while the sweet smell of gardenia
makes carnation pudding of my sweat
as it runs down the alleys of my skin
where I store the myth I've made of myself,
inside my skin, where I store

the mirror image of my doings
on this planet, where I experience
light as an explosion of hydrogen atoms
and as the heartbeat of tile universe
because on a sweet-hot summer day
I realized that the pulsation of my heartbeat
radiates order and discipline
to those who love me
that they feed off of my electricity
and I feed off of theirs,
>   fair exchanges in a swimming pool
>   full of chomping jaws,
>   take your time,
>   fast is slow,
>   slow is fast
>   and that's the way time goes.

Poems de Amor
(1978)

Love Gum

I will not tear your hair out,
if you stop chewing at my heart
as if it were bubble gum.

Sweetless Gum

Remember the day you unwrapped
me and found the sweet in me,
remember how you chewed till
all my sugar dissolved in your mouth
and do you remember
how you smiled, looked around
and stuck me like a juicy fruit
gum run out of flavor onto the chair
that you left behind at the Tin Palace?

Woman With Teeth

O.K.— I won't scream
but your teeth are scraping
my head raw and your touch
explodes like bombs of anger
and your tongue in my ear
has the roar of a storm bursting
my drums as you choke me
trying to thrust your five
fingers right down in to my stomach,
grabbing my lower colon and pulling
                    and pulling
till you've turned me inside out

exposing all of my organs,
you want to play with my liver
and bite at it,
you want to bite my thyroid
glands and get high on my adrenalin,
don't hide your teeth now
don't pull them in
cause you're getting down
to where I store what I can't digest,
don't give up now
let your teeth relieve me of my constipation,
bite my leftovers,
go ahead bubble gum chewer
suck the acrid, bitter poison
that destroys my inner-self,
go ahead, skin scraper,
nibble at me with your piranha teeth,
I won't scream.
not if you bite my pain away.

Nausea-Control

The other night we began to make love,
and I was rum sick,
mucho pot high,
and all the food in my belly
was trying to climb out of my gut,
I looked at you dizzy spinning,
took a deep breath
to hold down my vomit,
slipped my right hand
around your waist from left to right,
lifted your full weight,
turned you upside down
and as your legs peeled down
I took a face dive
into your wide open
mucous and cavernous cunt.

El Capitán San Miguelito, *Part One*
(1975)

Come home to East Sixth Street
To find war,
No ease, no space,
El Capitán San Miguelito
Is directing a new play
On the street corner
Wearing colors
Looking bad
Letting Avenue B know
It's on,
El Capitán San Miguelito
Is bored with nothing to do
With his coke pulse
Surging beneath his skin
Causing cataracts of martial
Art images to confound his muscles
Into convulsions,
Cane in hand
Head thrown back
Sleeveless denim jacket
Ornamented with Mr. Tee's
NUYORICAN POETS
Yin, Yang, Black liberation colors
And Puerto Rican flag emblem
On the back,
El Capitán San Miguelito
Stands there making subtle

Attacks, daring the Avenue
To get in his way,
"Come on Avenue B
Give me a complication,
Get in my way,
Bring me some trouble,
Take my boredom away,"
San Miguelito
Is heard every day saying
His prayers on the B-way—
Mira lo que pasó los otros días,
El Capitán
Was standing on the corner
Styling with his profile
All fine and bien tirao
When I passed by in my
'67 Firebird
I blew the horn and waved
San Miguelito raised his cane
And as he gave salute poking the air
The sun was heard to sigh
In envy of San Miguelito's colors,
El Capitán shone so bright that
The B-way was a ruby
Glistening bright
But he was bored
And out on the street
With nothing to do
With his coke pulse
When up came a play
It was Angel on the run
Fleeing through El Capitán's
Concrete garden
Up came the cane pointing

At Angel who like a fury
Of fear was rushing in and out
Of building entrances
Trying to avoid the steel bullet
Searching to make love
To his heart
Up came the cane again
Looking to assuage
El Capitán's boredom
And there started the play,
"Get a gun, a kid's been shot
And the Renigades are fighting
The whole third world uptown."
Serious, deadly words grew
From the bored coked forked tongue of
El Capitán San Miguelito,
The village people listened
Opened their feelings
To receive and to connect
With the urgent drive
That suddenly possessed
El Capitán,
People stood at attention
Ready
Eager to act
At the moment of hearing
El Capitán's words—
Everybody bared their trust
And on came the words
"Angel, get a gun and meet me
At Miguel's ready to move,
Miguel get the car going,
Mr. Tee secure another gun
And the station wagon,

George, Lil Man, Cheo
Move to the back of the car
Prepare to rumble tonight,"
The whole village watched the fire
Of his presence as he ordered
Young and old Nuyoricans
Into battle
"Prepare to have life and love
Flow out of your bodies
As you protect the Renigades tonight,"
There was pride in the people
Who were asked to fly on wings
Of brick dreams to protect the
Renigade nation from aggression
As the heat intensified
San Miguelito's boredom loosened
Its grip and his psyche flew on
Wings of gratitude as his pinky
Shoveled crystal grains of thanks
Into his driver's nose;
There was direction, tension, attention,
Action, there was action
To dissolve the tension of boredom,
There was action
To intrigue the hole of nothingness
Into interest
There was motion-pleasure in
El Capitán San Miguelito's
Eyes as he sailed in the wind
Of the east river going north
To the troubled, rumbling
Renigade nation
Young Nuyorican warriors
To his right and rear

Trusting El Capitán's clarity
As he coordinated people energy
Into risking all and life
For the Renigades' safety,
The drive brought us together
Into a mix of passions and a will
To fight that brews among men
When their right to freedom
Is brought to the point of armed struggle
In the tar jungle of Manhattan,
El Capitán San Miguelito
Was voyaging north miles away
From Nuyorican Village home ground
Away into alien East Harlem
Concrete sidewalks where the law
Of survival wears different colors
And different motives for killing,
El Capitán's armored car left the
East River Drive at 125th St.,
Turned left underneath the Triboro Bridge
Cruised west to Second Ave.,
Turned left, headed south to 119th St.,
Turned right, parked on the northwest
Corner of the Ave.,
The station wagon pulled in 30 seconds
Behind us,
El Capitán was the first to step on alien
Territory, all eyes were on him as he
Brandished his colors, struck pose,
Tapped cane, motioned for the canvas sack
With weapons and gave orders for
The men in the first car to leave car,
San Miguelito having shown strength
Reinforces his presence and with a

Poke from his cane gives orders
For the men in the station wagon to leave car,
El Capitán announces himself as he walks
Straight to the Supreme President
Of the Renigades of Harlem
And embraces and gives greetings
Of love and support from the people of
Nuyorican Village,
The young ghetto warriors
Respond only to El Capitán's orders,
They wait for a sign
No sign is given
They wait for action
No sign is given
The mood uptown is mellow
High and rich in feelings
The newly renovated building
Shines bright like newly polished shoes,
The young Nuyorican bloods
Are received with love
And at this moment there is no war—
There could have been war an hour ago,
There could be war minutes after we leave,
But there is no war going on,
Yet we come armed,
Ready to fight,
Armed, armed
For bloody struggle,
El Capitán San Miguelito
Smiles and sheds good vibes
Packing his rod next to his
Belly button, he oozes
Cheer and crystal grains from
Left to right making all

Eyes glow as his rainbow presence
Passes by,
The Supreme President asks the
Nuyoricans into the building
To look at the 2001 renovated
Spaceship that they had labored
To put together while a hostile
Police Department and New York
City Housing Authority struggled
To prove them wrong,
El Capitán went down the stairs
Into the basement where a dated
Gun with missing parts was given
To the Supreme President,
Electrical joy circulated
As the weapon reached the
Renigade nation, one gun—
For which the Nuyorican warriors
Had risked love and life
To flow out of their bodies
To bring here their mission
Accomplished here it was—done,
One sawed-off gun, parts missing,
Had provoked armed intervention
Into alien territory,
El Capitán was exultant, his boredom
Undone.

El Capitán San Miguelito, *Part Two*
December 8, 1975

8:30 a.m. and I wake up to
the rhythms of my telephone
and El Capitán's fugitive voice
rapping on about having arrived
from where he's hiding
cause he put his inhibitions to the wind
and insulted all our street
army trained leaders:
> no really!
> he did insult
our hearts but then again he didn't care
whether our love bled on the tar
or the concrete of Nuyorican Village
where El Capitán creates sidewalk
dramas that cause our sentimental registers
to groan loud red complaints against his
betrayal of our street government trust:
"¿Capitán coma estás negro?"
"I just got into town,
estoy en la casa de Pancho,"
"Óyeme, keep cool,"
"Miguel, I've never been so afraid,"
"Are you enjoying it?"
"No, I really mean it,
I'm afraid,"
"Oye, I'll see you tonight
in the light booth,"

"Listen, I don't want anybody
to know that I am here,"
El Capitán sounded tired without
space as if caught in a thick wave
of self-created paranoia where to feel
fear is the cure for guilt and leaves
you free to still move on creating
more chaos in people's hearts as they
open their love and throw caution
out to pasture on concrete sidewalks
while you, our Capitán, sink infected needle-
sharp spurs into our heart-muscle
as you gallop through
our streets shitting and pissing
in our faces without compassion for our
shame and hurt, oye, Capitán,
when we saw your rising star we thought
we'd all be born again and we were
because your generosity has the thickness
of a tenor sax riffing to the creator
about the width of our spreading New York ghetto
plague as you write celestial concrete poetry
to los dioses de la palabra,
we see and we saw your beauty
so why pull midnight horror shows
on us and on the B-way when you can
spread the pure breath of beauty
oye, Capitán, sin ti no hay otro
                    sin ti no hay teatro,
without you there is no "barely filtered"
reality because no one here lives to the raw
like you do burning up your energies
without preservation for tomorrow constipation,
you pulled an army of young street heroes

into a bunch of futuristic hope, so a man
has a right to falter, to victimize himself,
to desire more than his player-card can stand
and to fall hopeless, there, on the street,
disappearing into the cracks of the sidewalk,
a man has a right to be humiliated
so he can walk upright again
confronting the verbs and adjectives
of people that tongue-lash his freedom
and shatter his ego into razor sharp shards
that cut into his feelings and into his muscles
and into his sleep, Capitán, you also have a right
to work your fears out and to be resisted
when your will's too weak,
                                too meek
to strike back with war and grenades,
                                too meek
to resist the acid stare and glare
of people's bared, daring street blare
against your thereness, your ghostly duality,
                                Capitán,
we wait upon your strength and when there's none
we give unto your strength what you don't have at
that minute, more power for you to beat
merciless desire from eating your manhood,
yo deseo, tu deseas, nosotros deseamos,
that's the truth of your choices and
it is all we know about envy,
                envy makes people destroy,
                oh querido Capitán green is
                for life and green is for atomic
                evil directed at your heart because
                you've gone beyond where we all
                stand on concrete ground

holding an ice cream cone to soothe the
evil taste of melting flesh and broiled
white lies about not being able
to wait out the night till morning break
sends a new day to frighten us into trying
again what we forgot to do yesterday
which was the day before that
       and now we're here
       in a presence that is not
       about where you've been
       but where you are
ay, ay, ay, ay, ay, ay
mi amigo, my queso jones
keep coming down,
       watch out I'll spark you up,
            I'll spark you up,
            I'll spark you up,
watch out or I'll spark and squash
the budding fire of your springtime
ignorance, not knowing quite what
it is that you are doing to bring
about consequences that force you to the gallows where
men hang from their necks till sperm
swims up to plead their case,
       "oh please let me find a cavern
       that will make me plenty
       strong and body full,"
Oye, Capitán, Eddie Conde beats the
timbales into molten steel rims
and resonating centerskin—
when the elementary rhythm of God
was born you smiled because you
recognized him and yourself in him
so why not give us full timing

of space and of mind as you share your
fullest self with us,
            Oye, Capitán,
I'm left with a tooth ache
            and a belly ache
            and a stomach ache
when I can make no contact
            with your full faced self,
while Barbara's cold shoulder
shivers anger at me
as she gives her back to my smile
and breaks a major not a minor rule
"Nobody ever gives his or her back to the bar"
yet there she is insulting
all and me in her angry
claim that Richie and I don't know
who our friends are because when
people wouldn't shut up for her reading
I didn't get pissed off at the women
who were talking through her reading
and my reading of Archie's poem
about his father's death in Vietnam,
Barbara didn't get to read because
she was playing it like a kinder-
garten Marm who looks over her
spectacles at the class as she waits
for SILENCE! meanwhile, we,
us, you, I the tribe of ignoramuses that
we are, we keep rapping and enjoying
ourselves and talking and burping and
farting till our school Marm Barbara
fills the environment with venom
and confusion and her pain—,
it's disastrous to be caught in angry

woman territory without a minor weapon
to defend a major claim of hurt
and betrayal as Barbara's liberation rap
whips up creamy shit vibes,
and Carmen reads liberation literature
        from the freaky creatures
whose pens spit out left-wing propaganda,
a Communist Leninist rap that moves a mile per breath
but really Carmen's heart's bent on your mouth
        and your tongue is the balm
            that would soothe her light thighs
and her lips and her everything else,
I think she comes close to the coming
at the mention of your anything
        —mira, Capitán,
yo te quiero y por ti sueño
en lo que eres y lo que serás
and over my trigueña soledad
you've poured the honey of
a warrior's joy and into my memories,
images of our past and our present
rush in, but for now I look at Carmen's deep
penetrating eyes and I read the
hurt that is not me but that is her
pain in your absence,
        mira, Capitán,
sweet butter melts into the electrical
field of action that is between our synapses
as I drown in an ice cream ocean
that chokes my breath with torrents of sweet
liquid Hershey chocolate and Breyer's peached cream,
I, we, you, us, the US of us
drowns in an ocean of chemical carbohydrates
that shorten our lives, widen our girth

and overtax our hearts,
       no, señor,
       sí, señor,
       oye, señor,
when white uniformed surgeons holding
a scalpel in hand come to deliver me
of death send them away,
don't let them cut holes in my mind-body,
       mándalos al carajo
and hold my hand until my last breath
gives way and I fall dead in your
fugitive hands,
       do not betray me to the surgeon's knife
       instead take me gently to the volcano's
       edge and let me fall off the precipice
       without, and I remind you, the surgeon's knife
cutting into my body to deliver me from pain
while creating a newer pain that dries
my will to live to the max as Eddie
beats the conga skin to red hot rhythms,
       hay algo,
       hay algo,
       hay algo,
       mi Capitán.

Inside Control
(1978)

There's a hand on the scruff
          of my neck: there's a vise
that compresses the nerves
          to my brain skin, there is
pressure constant, celebrating
          itself, inculcating a tension
beneath my cranium there is
          a whip of nine lashing
tails finely decorated with
          thousands of miniscule pins
on each end, lacerating,
          eating away at my neurological
cells, there is a tyranny against
          my functioning mind: I am
programmed to revolt: the
          program eradicates all
disposition to rest still,
          inside.

Not Tonight but Tomorrow
(1978)

Not tonight but tomorrow
when the light turns the peach
tree green and the Earth sprouts
its young leaves looking to repeat
the magical mystery tour of
photosynthetic conversion of light
and moisture into life—
Not tonight but tomorrow
when my body will have shed
its fear of turning old and soft
will I turn my speeding mind
into the tunnels of your psyche
to melt the calcium that constipates
your synapses into a lubricating powder—
Not tonight but tomorrow
when the Universe moves on
beyond the field of action
that is Earth to me and you
will I discover interplanetary clues
that signal the roots of my moment to you—
Not tonight but tomorrow
will I throw my feelings into
New York streets to stew
in the violence and despair
of our planet—
Not tonight but tomorrow
will the Earth turn green again.

A Salsa Ballet: *Angelitos Negros*
(1978)

Willie Colón, Composer
Marty Sheller, Conductor

2 trumpets
1 trombone
2 saxophone / alto and baritone
1 bass
1 piano
1 guitar
1 trap drum
1 bongo
1 Conga
1 timbalero
6 violins
1 flute and piccolo

Prologue
Good Vibrations Sound Studio,
the date is for three
but we arrived at 2:30 p.m.,
the occasion: the first recording
of Willie Colón's score of "A Salsa Ballet":
the studio is refrigerator cool,
the vibes are mellow,
the rhythm is sleepy slow,
the set is slowly pulling together,
musicians arrive, slapping hands
talking through months of absence

into hugs and tightly held hands,
they are coming together
to invent
the sound that Willie
has in his head,
musicians are Willie's brush,
musicians are Willie's sound partners,
today's the day for an orgy of sounds,
today is the day for the birth
of a new Latin perception
of sound,
Willie walks around,
four months into his pregnancy,
I see prenatal rhythmic juices pour
out of his pores as notes shoot
pitches of sounds high into the atmosphere,
musicians come together in a holy
trust, the bond of marriage for
a trumpet and a saxophone
is in the listening
that they do to one another,
there in the listening,
there is hope.

Take One

Jon Fausty engineers
the recording machine,
his hands control the sound
that is recorded,
what people hear
is the selection and balances
that he invents at his electronic
keyboard,
the heat is rising,

the ears are hot,
attention is total,
the blend is on and as
everybody listens
the salsa melts individuality,
the flow is clear sound,
every instrument can be distinguished,
the Latin beat is on electronic
tape.

Take Two
"Hey Marty, let's put one
on from the top,
I haven't done one yet,"
Marty shakes his head
"O.K."
Take two: trap drummer
is added,
Marty beats out
basic rhythms,
the drummer riffs as he
plays into recording track.

Take Three
The piccolo player argues
that the ear cans are too loud,
"lower the ear phones,"
the take starts but Mauricio
stops it,
"still too loud,"
Jon,
"still too loud?"
Mauricio,
"Yes."

Jon,
"I'll turn them down."
Willie,
"wait, wait, wait,
he's got to do the bomba."
Marty,
"yes, wait."
The take is played,
Marty asks Mauricio
if he wants to hear
the solo—he nods yes.
Jon asks the drummer,
"is there anything you need in your ear?"
drummer,
"yeah, a little more bell."
Alfonso listens to the tape,
feels the rhythms,
lets loose
and moves deep into
the salsa, till he releases
his rhythms and drum talks
his soul to the tape.
Mauricio takes up the flute,
listens for another count,
then plays into the tape what Willie has
in his head—and it is
clear that the other
mind here is the electronic
composer that Jon is engineering.

Take Four
Four violins
two cellos
have been prepared

for electronic digestion
and integration onto
master-minded
Master Tape
"phones on the way Martin,"
Jon puffs his Kool,
jumps out of his chair,
runs out for the phones
comes back, looks around,
spins his chair, checks the
temperature, pushes start,
Marty motions,
"I want to run it through
once before we take,"
Jon understands,
the take begins but Marty's
running fast,
Willie stops the take,
"Marty it's really half of that."
Jon plays with the quality
of the sound as he searches
for a brassy violin tone,
Jon's balance is a treble
pitched violin that's almost
square dance Nuyorican salsa
electronically conceived.
Jon,
"Marty don't count aloud,"
the string players are excited,
one of them looks up astonished,
"hey, you've got a lot of heavy stuff
on that tape,"
Willie smiles and suggests,
"Marty why don't you direct,"

"that's what I'm doing," Marty says,
he directs a take,
looks up, face full of sweat,
"let's take a break,"
string players reject the break,
"let's do it again," they say,
Marty comes into the control booth,
Mauricio suggests that the horns
be taken out of the can,
it's done and the string players feel
it's easier so the take is final
and the string players leave
joyous,
Marty comes into the control booth,
Jon starts from the top and as the
tape plays Marty shakes Jon
on the shoulders and says,
"Pisces produce,"
Jon smiles as George, the young blood
that works for them, slaps
Jon five because he's Pisces too.

Take Five
Yomo Toro comes next,
here comes el cuatrito
de los Nuyoricans,
aquí viene Yomo Toro
Puerto Rico,
Yomo's next but first he
makes a call,
he's watched it all
and now comes Yomo,
he records the prelude
of the ballet,

Willie asks him for something
"más ajibarao."
Yomo grounds the chords
in Nuyorican salsa as
Willie calls out,
"algo bien cabrón"
Yomo says,
"no me jodas Willie
manda un violín."
Yomo is master cuatrista
showing his pleasure
in calling his
performance, "un concierto,"
Willie agrees to the last take
and the tape is moved to the
bomba and Yomo listens
before doing a take,
the rhythm moves in as Willie
sings it and Yomo tries,
Yomo says to Willie
"Oye vente tú aquí
y cántame el totín totín ese,"
Willie leaves the electronic capsule
and begins
"totín, totín
totín, totín."
Yomo shifts chords transforming
el cuatro into a classical rap
and today a salsa ballet
has just been put on
the face of the planet
Earth.

Trampling
(1980)

You take a woman,
force her to yield
and not too swiftly
but to resist
just enough to need
your macho force,
you rouse yourself by subjugating her,
you get it hard
and make her
eat meat totally,
you enter her like molten steel
scorching her insides raw
as she refuses to consent
you rage in your macho savagery
by pounding blows all over her body,
till you've trampled the woman in her,
leaving her angry and frightened of men.

Baby food
(1980)

she gave birth,
gave out with child,
she bore it nine months
before contractions pushed it out
into New York,
                  she'd been hospitalized
for six days,
was glad to get out,
went home,
found she'd left her money at the clinic,
got desperate,
ran back out,
but first she lay her baby down,
came back home
and found that her German Shepherd,
six days into starvation,
had chewed her baby to pieces,
its innards splattered over the floor
her dog had had its meal.

"Always throw the first punch"
(1980)

My uncle always insisted,
"strike the first punch,
put your enemy on the run,"
I always threw the first punch,
I remember,
"attack, attack, attack,
put the hurting
on his limbs,"
I remember,
I remember
the night my uncle
got angry because I said
his wife thought his nuts
were christmas walnuts
and that she cracked them
every day of the year,
his left arm twitched,
I leapt at him
and struck first.

Ray Barretto: December 4, 1976

Eddie Conde, congas
Edwina, congas
Richie Cruz, timbales & congas,
trio of intense rhythmic improvisation,
mobilizing muscle energy to pleasure,
as Barretto articulates
the pain of being artist in need of fair recognition,
he looks out and delivers medicine
to ears that follow the rhythmic clear talk
he gives out with the prac-ca-ta of his voice,
Barretto maestro,
Barretto, maestro to futuristic people
who have wakeful dreams for breakfast
and soured-up imagination for supper,
daylight is a long Star Trek episode
that matures to ripe old age by day's end,
Eddie, Edwina, Richie
mystical musicians inventing
patterns tailored to desire,
breaking through the present tension precision
into salsa root sinceridad,
Barretto maestro,
listening to Eddie, Edwina, Richie,
paying respect with your ears,
just like they learned your manhood through their ears,
Barretto, Doctor of Body Motion,
you release the monster that chews
the working man from inside out,

la gente se menea con tu ritmo,
sus músculos sudan cansancio,
sobre el piso que los zapatos limpian
según bailan tu música,
Barretto, yo he visto un baile entero,
un baile de 20,000 personas
en Madison Square Garden,
respirar como si fueran una sola persona,
no miles, pero un solo corazón boricua,
Barretto, maestro del working class,
when you arrived at the Nuyorican Poets' Café
our hearts swung open for you as we made way
for your centered presence,
qué limpio tú estás,
no static in your pure intent of love.

September 11, 1977 Day of Birth

Born on this day thirty-six years ago,
eyes moving deciphering coded signals
that invade the nostrils of the mind,
the moment begins in faltering,
where we sing to la diosa
together to get her into the web
of feeling communication
that restores a black Cuban woman's memory,
her soprano soaring low inside her throat,
two violins loving the virgin's ear,
ayudan with gentle songs that glue
our feelings to Tato's sleepy 2:30 Sunday
afternoon I'll be there meaning four
hours later voice, la negra en amarillo
canta débilmente pero el intento está claro,
Pito whistles boredom's stars and stripes,
instead of la Santa he'd rather see Star Wars,
no importa, no matter, no hay nada,
no se apure, no hay miedo,
yo lo dejo en Star Wars
y me voy a ver la Santa,
si es que Cachita la baja,
aunque Ruth con todo su poder
la bajaría a palos morales si fuese necesario
ella que lo ha trabajado,
que lo ha hecho a puro esfuerzo,
la tarde bella, despejada, alejada,
Pito mirando la pluma dejar

su tinta azul sobre el papel blanco
dejando el intento de mis sentimientos
en esta tarde azul, cantando a la virgen
sin pecado original,
que ayuda aquí y ayuda allá,
las venas negras y trigueñas
que conducen la sangre a
manos que peinan y estiran
el pelo de los maniseros que van,
esperando, esperando que el cantar
de los congos llegue,
congo, conguito baja a la tierra
a hacer caridad,
no nos desampare, danos caridad,
a remar, a remar,
no dejemos de remar,
hasta llegar al yunque de Ruth
y allí disfrutar de su humildad,
baila, Ruth, baila,
salir a Dios, bailando a Dios,
baila, sal, baila,
da vueltas, no dejes de virar,
mirar, gritar, salir a Dios,
resucitar la intención original,
que viva Changó, que viva Changó,
que viva Changó, señores.

Broadway opening
(1980)

Ntozake Shange's Broadway opening
and Melvin Van Peeble's saying
that his T.V. special last night
"was so good it
should've been a series,"
Amiri Baraka
sits proudly passing his
Unity Struggle newspaper
to partying black folk
who're celebrating Ntozake's
Grand Ole Opry opening
into full theatrical success,
as she leaps at love
like a street mountain cat,
eight minutes standing ovation
but Ntozake is still as raw
and full of hurt
as she was before and after
her words threw fire
into New York's theater jungle.

Richard Directs Lucky's Flamingo
(1980)

Richard realizes self,
he comes to life in the light
of the certain truth of changingness,
the purity of realizing self
which is feeling what's concrete
in flesh and steel
like flamingoes flaming
into August colors, actual
                    touching
                    Rosa red,
Atsuko pink and Frankie soft blue,
        ¡oye mi nuevo guagancó!
what's the pain prince of control?
doctor of the streets of New York
who handles dynamite as if it were
a common cold distressing
yet neither pungent pain/nor red depression/
August sun August in aspect
I wish that I had had the have to have
the best of myself in your presence
all the time that you and I
planned to plan just what's to be,
prince of selfless love
offer yourself full pleasure
and trust the whereabouts
you've been with me
cause there is nothing other

than what we've made,
prince of cool continuity
and sincere perseverance
I began to see
when you offered me air
and space to lung myself
into being in the presence
of your watchful,
sparing self,
        and now
you realize your self,
Amalivaca, god of the winds
of invention,
        in your old form,
keeping time with yourself,
inventing your shape
from day to day
growing into and out of
the planet poeta
the supreme fiction is in the making of it,
in the balancing of object and will,
in the centering of self
right in the middle of the onrush
face to face with chaos,
square in the mouth of the lion
your monster grows,
leaps, rushes, strikes,
whirls midair,
foams at the mouth
and as balance conquers anger
you connect again
into cool, blue continuity
and thick green love.

Taos Pueblo Indians: 700 strong
according to Bobby's last census
(1980)

It costs $1.50 for my van to enter
Taos Pueblo Indian land,
adobe huts, brown tanned Indian red skin
reminding me of brown Nuyorican people,
young Taos Pueblo Indians
ride the back of a pickup truck
with no memories of mustangs
controlled by their naked calves and thighs,
rocky, unpaved roads, red brown dirt,
a stream bridged by wide trunk planks,
young warriors unloading thick trunks
for the village drum makers to work,
tourists bringing the greens,
Indian women fry flour and bake bread,
older men attend curio shops,
the center of the village is a parking lot
into which America's mobile homes
pour in with their air-conditioned cabins, color
T.V., fully equipped kitchens, bathrooms
with flushing toilets and showers,
a.m. & f.m. quadrophonic stereo sound,
cameras, geiger counters, tents,
hiking boots, fishing gear and mobile telephones,
"restricted" signs are posted round the parking lot
making the final stage for the zoo
where the natives approach selling

American jewelry made in Phoenix
by a foster American Indian from Brooklyn
who runs a missionary profit-making turquoise jewelry shop
"Ma, is this clean water?
do the Indians drink out of this water?
is it all right for me to drink it?"
the young white substitute teacher's daughter
wants to drink some Indian water,
young village school children recognize her,
and in her presence the children snap
quick attentive looks that melt into
"boy am I glad I'm not in school"
gestures as we pass,
but past, past this living room zoo,
out there on that ridge,
over there, over that ridge,
on the other side of that mountain,
is that Indian land too?
are there leaders and governments over that ridge?
does Indian law exist there?
who would the Pueblo Indian send
to a formal State meeting
with the heads of street government,
who would we plan war with?
can we transport arms earmarked for ghetto
warriors, can we construct our street
government constitutions on your land?
when orthodox Jews from Crown Heights
receive arms from Israel in their territorial struggle
with local Brooklyn Blacks,
can we raise your flag
in the Lower East Side
as a sign of our mutual treaty of protection?
"hey, you, you're not supposed to walk in our water,"

"stay back we're busy making bread,"
these were beside your "restricted zones"
the most authoritative words
spoken by your native tongue,
the girl's worry about her drinking water
made Raúl remove his Brazilian made shoes
from the Pueblo Indian drinking cup,
the old woman's bread warning
froze me dead on the spot
"go buy something in the shop,
you understand me, go buy something,"
I didn't buy I just strolled on by the curio shops
till I came across Bobby the police officer,
taught at Santa Fe, though he could've gone on to Albuquerque,
Taos Pueblo Indians
sending their officers of the law to be trained
in neighboring but foreign cities like in New Mexico
proves that Taos Pueblo Indians
ignore that a soldier belongs to his trainer
that his discipline, his habitual muscle response
belongs to his drill sergeant master:
"our laws are the same as up in town"
too bad Bobby! they could be your laws,
it's your land!
then flashing past as I leave Taos Bobby speeds
towards the reservation in a 1978 GMC van with two red flashers
on top bringing Red Cross survival rations to the Taos Pueblo Indians
respectfully frying bread for tourists
behind their sovereign borders.

Sylvester's "Step II"
(1980)

"Will you please step aside,"
Sylvester's balloon's passing by,
yellow, blue, red, flaming orange
San Francisco disco hero passing
through chicly rust colored English tweed,
aviator hat and glasses framing
black mustache, brown pimply skin,
disco beat, pulsating, distressing,
pretty people Carol Burnett,
bucked teeth and skinny,
pinstriped suited Billy Dee Williams
black matinee idol nausea,
balloons suspended from a twenty-foot
ceiling ambush Community Speakers,
horns accompanied by three floor
basses, oh Nuyorican salsa
disco madness, John Travolta
danza craze,
Lobo's *Latin Hustle Dance Contest*
contemporary bomba, plena happiness,
oh solitude
dressed in tight blackness,
oh pleasure of
ohing,
oh, oh, of oh,
"dance to the beat of the disco beat,"
Sylvester's push to the disco beat,

his pierced diamonded ear
enveloping the nation in:
"dance to the beat of the disco beat,"
his impatient twist of relaxed
black American curls,
his black, Lobo's black,
twist of the disco beat,
sign your autographs, Sylvester,
Eddie knew you'd be here in ten minutes,
"how ya doing Sylvester,"
"Fine, Fine,"
"Fine, good, that's fine,"
dance, *Dance! Dance!*
Dance! Sylvester
to the beat of the disco beat,
(Sylvester kissed my hand
when I told him I was writing
a poem about him)
spinning disco percussive lights,
hand clapping slick, khaki bucks
on Willie, black, blackly, black,
black Miguel,
oh Halloween,
hallow as tween solitary sheets
divided by one set of muscles
"dance to the beat of the disco heat,"
dance, dance, dance,
Eddie Rivera host,
Eddie Rivera visionary disco cultist,
stripping public school Nuyoricans
of repressions
let them dance,
dance, dance as Sylvester
beats his beat to the disco heat,

"is it not or is it not Latin music,"
black, blackly dressed Lobo
asks bending over with sunkist
Florida orange drink swimming in tingling, melting
ice cubes,
let them dance,
Eddie Rivera inventor,
Willie Correa disc spinner
as Nuyorican men dance free form
around their souls as the grooved wax spins
out Sylvester's "Step II"
while Nuyorican dance warriors
keep clave to the beat of the disco beat,
Poets'
Café
Commanding
CENTER SPACE
for dark Taíno junior priest
to spin trigueña juices flowing free
for Eddie and Sylvester to share,
rust shirt banged Taíno
Sylvester's San Francisco
jaunt into Halloweened New York
ends,
dance
dance
to the beat
of the disco
heat.

Rome: Santa María In Trastevere
(1982)

Part I
Rome, I see you again

Rome, I see you again,
Santa María!
No Nuke Sperm Here,
can't afford 25,000 years
of cellular radioactivity,
Santa María in Trastevere
plaza where eyes rove
till mutual contact
explodes the raw uranium
of flesh on flesh risk,
after love and dangerous deposits
there's falling hair,
rotting teeth and marrow cancer,
after love our lips
develop sores and drip nuclear pus,
Santa María!
running off to Casa Blanca
for transexual liquidation of Hermaphrodite.
muse inspired in both sexes,
Keats died looking out a window,
Shelley helped him storm
the citadel of heaven,
he spitting rancid blood
as Shelley telegrammed the angels
to prepare heavens jubilation
at his coming and conversion

to spirit matter,
flashing eight to thirteen flicks
per second
inner world matter,
Keats perceiving through feverish
hallucinations,
             through blood
spat up to accommodate oxygen,
Rome, I see you again,
             I
             see
you again
             I
             breathe
you again
             I
feel your hieroglyphics give way,
upstream to my insistent paddle,
coming to perceive,
             to inhale
sleep and poetry
as the day goes perilously on its way,
upstream against the planetary round
the earth makes every twenty-four hours;
      "IN THIS ROOM
      ON THE 23RD OF FEBRUARY 1821
             DIED
      JOHN KEATS"
and now wanting my dreams
draws me to a dream machine
where I'll yield two hundred years
of dreams not had to Rome,
of dreams fueled out of her gravity,
out of her present air pressure
where I'm helped up to God's window

to cut with Brian's flickering machine
God's barbed wire fence around my brain,
a fence Brian would tear with flickers,
    if he could,
paura,
      A NUCLEAR FLICKERING GOD,
25,000 years of mutations,
    APOCALYPSE,
"Hitler knew," says Brian,
"that's why he paid for Von Braun's space travel,"
deporting to new no oxygen grounds
nightmare robots he called "gifted man,"
a nuclear waste deposit fueled MAN,
pumping plutonium blood,
circulating mutations,
producing alien textures,
Rome, Roma, I,
see you again
through alpha waves eight to thirteen
flicker per second in Rome,
love gotten, not gotten,
got to get more oxygen, fly,
board space-age oil refinery at Ostia
commandeered by a Burroughs computer
instructed to destroy crew
in favor of new worlds
in which to breed,
in which to sow
new grounds for perpetuating
earthly images of ourselves,
mutated space age man
bent on speaking to the whole,
not a part, but the whole assemblage
at II Premiere Festival del Poeti at Ostia.

Part II

Betty Carter at the Villa Borghese Gardens

She medium for sound
she knowing no muscle resistance:
"did you hear that note,
it was an E,"
"no an F^b in concert key,
came just like that,"
she ancient Roman aqueduct
for sound flow,
she transparent meditations on a sax,
she the future of language,
direct to body, affecting
chemical, biological change,
emitting sounds at the door
of the beginning
    where
    sound is chemistry,
she no idea about the thing but the very thing itself,
she the moment,
she emotion,
she no fear of what's to come,
she improvisation itself,
she the answer to plutonium,
she a Roman bell
sounding off the liquid passage of time,
she invisible to secrets,
she melts psychic knots
through psychoanalytic scats,
she bass,
she piano,
she more flexible than wind.
she the spirit of Superwoman
in the American Dream,
"say B., you doing a set with Ray in Atlantic City,"
"no, he's still skating round that,"

she flows like Suzanne Farrell moves
in Balanchine's *Concerto Barroco*,
she spins saliva castles,
she cements the stars into a continuity,
like total orgasm after struggling
to break molds, to stray free,
right from the throat,
    seeking,
    yielding,
    weeping,
move vocal chords, out reach the piano,
    moving
    flowing
    giving
she cataracts of sublime scales,
    groping,
    touching,
she la musica.
she è una donna.
she meravigliosa.

Part III
He walks in beauty

He walks in beauty,
talking with the Voodoo man,
barking with the Shaman,
turning moss, churning,
poking at waste, discovering
paths that pull together
pointing a way to the future,
he walks, talks in beauty,
strolling with the Shaman,
seeking, peeking into dark holes,
where the light of his eyes strangles darkness,
leaving stark, cold facts:
He and the Voodoo man walking fields of medicinal herbs.

Part IV
You and me

You and me,
no images for you,
no metaphors about
digestion of radioactive love,
me and you in me,
you and me in you,
no (t)reason just reason,
mere tricky, sequential
genetical flows.

Part V
Just let me lick it

Just let me lick it,
am not entering,
just massage your muscles,
it'll feel good,
will not push-it-in,
just lick it, kiss it,
breathe! don't stop,
feel pleasure,
feel pleasure,
give up your macho,
let him escape in Rome,
cut him loose,
dump him,
don't carry him anymore,
hell turn you hunch-backed,
breathe! don't stop,
feel pleasure in pressure
let me pry you open with meat.

Portraits
(1982)

XII
Body Bee calling love

Body Bee calling love:
transmitting a meeting,
Body Bee calling love:
afraid of the swelling,
a fear of hardness enduring,
a fear of an end during flight,
Body Bee calling love:
distress is in sight,
snooping into the certain death
of a bird's broken flight,
grounded on tar and concrete, flapping,
seeking shelter amid city weeds,
staring at its desperate eyes
I signal no danger from me,
letting feelings zoom into its dying effort,
I peer into its camouflage
among Bruckner Boulevard service road weeds,
wing bone shining in late August light,
wing flapping like broken American flags
torn by the acid corruption of state,
leaving me to transmit a meeting
calling for the one in two or the two of one
or the I in you or the you in me,
letting you know you're loved
snooping in, unsettling silence,
sensual waves transporting

I/eye and bird/eye into soothing blue
spiked by exposed bone seeking shelter
here . . .

XIII
A void

A void
Avoid
A void is something to avoid,
it's hard to be at zero point
at the still point reflecting the whole
in that there isn't anything in nothing
just like a circle is all ways not flat
but rounder than a belly nine months
into that other eternal circle
around the biological/chemical time clock
measured accurately by Swiss-made
round face father Timex,
avoid a void at the still point
where no thing becomes some thing
in that it is out of nothing that something comes,
avoid a void with a circumference,
it's a circle around the zero point
where a straight line that never goes round
begins a voyage that avoids a void
and heads towards a swell.

XXXII
Materialization, March 22, 1982

Stopped cat-like to watch Nuyorican man
space out on intergalactic electronic war game,
our circuits matched, mental travellers
put temple at center, feel there!
at one with magic men more gentle than wind

who recognize each other at the silent door and
on opening it fall right through the floor
till they find a white sand mound
out of which pops a magic man
saying funny words about a curveless voyage.

XXXVII
Fiery saxophonist . . .

It is invisible in that it is always new,
forget, what's next? forget, what's next?
let moment be instance of action,
forgetting, you're forgetting
what's needed to ground 'round father time,
I forget, you forget,
he's forgetting, we're forgetting,
we're for getting the round of a whole
that's in parts,
Body Bee is for getting a signal
terrestrial in source about us,
the U.S. of us,
the U.S. Shuttle to Space and us,
is there anybody sparking?
score, store till signal is restored,
signals propounding what's to be,
signals reporting what is being seen,
signs recording what has been
in visible but unregarded space,
the future is without distinctions,
a thickening, deadening, roarless growth.

XXXVIII
Dematerialization

Let go into a certain sweetness,
an embracing warmth,

a clean, well-lighted space station of the mind,
a regarded place through which coheres the impulse
to hold on in the act of letting go,
in pure visibility to have pure invisibility
understanding that standing under roots,
obstructs the line that moves ahead,
hold tight!
if you want to make this feeling stay
do not let this moment fade,
hold tight!
try it out,
you can do it,
hit it hard! you are there!
leave a story people tell
cause you are marksman
hitting targets, drawing blood,
moving tongues,
so you wander, signifying,
moving on, having contact,
making meaning and while moving
hold on tight,
if you want to make this feeling stay,
help me! somebody help!
the mystery has been waiting long,
YES! I've come this way before,
but this feeling is strong
and this feeling is real,
see me and love yourself,
see me and see yourself,
letting go, embracing certain sweetness,
see yourself and see me
cross currents,
crisscrossing
just to make this feeling stay.

Relish
(1985)

I'm frightened by so much heat,
sweating so much desire, sliding,
greased by tenderness,
enduring the sensual whirlpool
of your lips moistened by mutual saliva,
your hands caressing
my juices, transforming them into flesh,
made of blood and sperm,
the only actual possibility
for desire become the gelatin
of you and me
writhing in the sea.

Sabrosura

Me da miedo sentir tanto calor,
sudar tanto deseo, resbalar,
engrasado por la ternura,
que perdura en el remolino sensual
de tus labios mojados con saliva mutua,
tus manos acariciando
mi sabrosura, convirtiéndola en carne,
construida de sangre y leche,
la única posibilidad actual,
del deseo hecho el tembleque
de tú y yo
estrujándonos en el mar.

Life
(1985)

What could be said about her?
except she's a hole,
and to be happy is to occupy that space,
since the world is for me,
not for anybody,
since there aren't any sincere folks,
even though those who comply exist,
carrying a harvest of brotherliness,
that consumes them
in a short life
where love is evil,
and warmth, the timid sweet
of an overwhelming bitterness.

La vida

¿Qué se podría decir de ella?
sino que es un roto,
y el estar alegre es el ocupar ese espacio,
ya que el mundo es para uno,
no para nadie,
ya que de los sinceros no hay,
aunque cumplidores se encuentran,
cargando su cosecha de hermandad,
que los consume
en una vida corta,
donde el amor es la maldad,
y el cariño, el tímido dulce
de una agridez total.

But with a difference
(1985)

Change arrives,
a new medicinal rhythm pulverizes pain,
I search the flow of a song
that surges for you, for me,
sweet melody that screams:
what's for me?
with change there's difference,
showing steps not taken,
offering kisses that begin to fill,
lips that start to nourish,
tongue that washes,
hands that relieve,
arms that embrace change without fear.

Pero con la diferencia

Llega el cambio,
y un nuevo ritmo medicinal pulveriza el dolor.
Busco la fuente de una canción
que surge para ti, para mí,
dulce melodía que grita:
"¿y para mí qué?"
Con el cambio llega la diferencia,
enseñándome pasos no dados,
ofreciendo besos que empiezan a llenar,
labios que llegan a nutrir,
lengua que lava,
manos que alivian,
brazos que abrazan el cambio sin miedo.

Fear
(1985)

They hear us, see us, they pursue us
into toilets, classrooms, stores
they spy on us pissing between parked cars
they peep every signal transmitted
they envy our private meditations
they wring every pure emotion out of us
born of our trust
they rape us with cable T.V.—the invisible spy—
transmitting while appearing to be off.
The cure cures us with procuring,
you're procured, I'm procured,
they procure us with the cure,
curing us in the midst of a battle
that destroys before the cure cures this pure lunacy.

Miedo

Ellos nos oyen, nos ven, nos persiguen
a los inodoros, a los salones, a las tiendas
nos notan toda señal transmitida
nos añoran nuestras meditaciones privadas
nos escurren cada gota de emoción pura
inspirada en nuestra confianza
nos violan con el espía invisible de la televisión por cable
que transmite cuando el ojo aparenta dormir.
La cura nos cura con la procura.
Te procuran, me procuran,
nos procuran con la cura,
curándonos en medio de una batalla
que destruye antes de que la cura cure esta pura locura.

Though there's a new prayer: first part
(to three cowboys)
(1985)

A new trinity arrives
in the name of Father Reagan,
of the Holy Spirit Haig
and the Son Weinberger, amen.
Tonight there's a religious act:
the meaning, eternal moment,
where the hillbillie leaves for the city,
dancing on down the road
to buy for his mom at the jewelers
the pearl of the seas, slave Borinquen,
free for six months, possessed for four hundred years,
giving it to his old lady,
who visualizes the Space Shuttle
taking and bringing the powerful,
leaving my parents in Queens,
where they die and live,
where my mother invents a thousand melodies
for the midday, light-orange
and pale, full of spume
that roll up on the mortal
sands of a city that sweats knives
of competition
between the Lord and his eternal Servant.
Already it's seen that the trinity ferments,
that lies dominate,
that the Japanese pay Allen off,
that Reagan equivocates,
at he splits into thirty pieces at once,
crucifying global trust,
that's how the divine trinity falters.

Aunque hay una nueva oración: primera parte
(a tres vaqueros)

Ha llegado una nueva trinidad,
en el nombre del Padre Reagan,
del Espíritu Haig
y del hijo Weinberger, amén.
Esta noche se celebra un acto sacramental,
el significado, eterno momento,
donde el jibarito sale para la ciudad,
bailando así por el camino,
hacia la joyería a comprarle a su madre
la perla de los mares, la esclava Borinquen,
libre por seis meses, poseída por cuatrocientos años,
regalándosela a su viejita,
la cual visualiza el Space Shuttle
saliendo y llevando a los poderosos,
dejando a mis padres en Queens
donde se mueren y viven,
donde mi madre se inventa miles de melodías
para el mediodía, anaranjadas
y pálidas, llenas de espumas
que se desbordan en la arena
mortal de una ciudad que suda cuchillas
de la competencia
entre el Señor y su eterno Servidor.
Ya se ve que la trinidad fomenta,
que la mentira domina,
que los japoneses le pagan a Allen,
que Reagan ya miente,
que revienta en treinta pedazos a la vez,
crucificando la confianza mundial,
así ya falla la divina trinidad.

Look at the first lesson: second part
(the newspapers)
(1985)

The Secretary of State Alexander Haig,
disturbed by Washington's gossip,
telephoned Jack Anderson attacking
certain White House aides
as guerrillas bombarding
the matrimony of trust between him and Mr. Reagan.
It's said Mr. Haig found himself
so perturbed
so hurt
so nettled
that the Secretary of State
made a late night phone call to Mr. Anderson
assuring him anxiously
of the firm, constant friendship
and confidence he enjoys with Mr. Reagan:
"No one will weaken it."
But meanwhile,
our cowboy, our Haig,
stirring up a vigorous campaign
dares to call his Chief Reagan
asking a thousand pardons for the bother
but giving orders to the Chief
to break his peace and rest in Camp David
and call Jack Anderson so that
the mortal lie
not reach the press,
that he is no longer wanted in the White House
and that they have him on a disappointment list
with a foot on a banana peel.

Fíjense en la primera lección: segunda parte
(los periódicos)

El Secretario de Estado Alexander Haig,
molesto por los bochinches de Washington,
telefoneó a Jack Anderson atacando a
ciertos ayudantes de la Casa Blanca
como guerrilleros bombardeando
el matrimonio de confianza entre él y el Sr. Reagan.
Se dice que el Sr. Haig se encontró
tan perturbado
tan herido
tan pullado
que el Secretario de Estado
hizo una llamada telefónica tarde en la noche
    al Sr. Anderson
ansiosamente asegurándole
la firme y constante amistad
y confianza que él goza con el Sr. Reagan:
"nadie la afligirá",
pero mientras tanto,
nuestro vaquero, nuestro Haig,
formando una campaña vigorosa,
se atreve a llamar a su Jefe Reagan
pidiéndole mil excusas por la molestia
pero dándole órdenes al jefe
que rompa su paz y descanso en Camp David
y llame a Jack Anderson, cosa de que
el embuste mortal
no salga a la prensa,
que a él ya no lo quieren en la Casa Blanca
y que lo tienen en la lista de los desnombrados,
con un pie sobre una cáscara de guineo.

While Morazán is on the evening news: first part
(1985)

El Salvador asphyxiates
while I'm into an infinite gaze
at the sprouting quarrel,
participating in events that by afternoon
become the content of the 7 o'clock news.
Today El Salvador occupies space
on the twelfth page of the *New York Post.*
There's a photo of Two Salvadorans
shooting at each other
because the fog created by Washington
blinds them, El Salvador burns,
the guerrillas have taken Morazán,
Haig doesn't know who to hug.
Should he give a hand to the guerrilla who's winning
or the military forces that are losing?
But the struggle changes every second.
Who to love is the White House dilemma
while El Salvador explodes.

Mientras Morazán se encuentra en las noticias de la tarde: primera parte

El Salvador se asfixia
mientras me encuentro viendo infinitamente
la riña en desarrollo,
participando en eventos que al atardecer
ya son el contenido de las Noticias de las Siete.
Hoy El Salvador ocupa espacio
en la página doce del *New York Post*.
Hay una foto de dos salvadoreños
disparando uno contra el otro
porque la tiniebla creada en Washington
los ciega, El Salvador quema,
los guerrilleros se apoderan de Morazán,
Haig ya no sabe a quién abrazar,
si darle la mano al guerrillero que ganando va
o al ejército que perdiendo está,
pero al segundo la batalla cambia.
A quién querer es el dilema de la Casa Blanca
mientras El Salvador explota.

Elections and . . . : second part
(1985)

"People go out to vote
but the guerrillas obstruct them."
That's what's said on Channel 4 in Manhattan.
On the 28th of March we're made to understand
that Democracy is being obstructed
by the left, "the guerrillas
fire against the Salvadoran people,"
but that chaos was invented in the White House
and it doesn't afflict the public in Chatatenango,
there aren't any guarantees
for the public to take hold of!
although some go out and vote pretending
that the machinery is not fraudulent,
that Duarte doesn't repress,
not withstanding that it's written in every man's bible,
that in El Salvador Christ has not yet
freed his folk.

Elecciones y . . . : segunda parte

"La gente sale a votar
y los guerrilleros lo impiden",
así se dice en el Canal 4 en Manhattan.
Nos dan a entender el 28 de marzo
que la Democracia está obstruida
por la izquierda, "el guerrillero
dispara contra el pueblo salvadoreño",
pero ese caos fue inventado en la Casa Blanca
y no aflige al público de Chatatenango.
¡No hay garantías!
para que el pueblo se entregue
aunque algunos salen a votar fingiendo
que no hay fraude en el proceso,
que Duarte no oprime,
no obstante, se lee en el evangelio cotidiano
que el Cristo salvadoreño no ha logrado
liberar a su pueblo.

A defiance
(1985)

England and Argentina are spoused,
tied by the long Atlantic rope.
Today the wives are hand-cuffed,
fighting and bombarding the Falklands,
looking for right of possession.
"The Falklands are mine,"
says Margaret.
"No, their ours,"
says Nicanor.
What shame!
So many die,
Latin America betrayed,
England protected,
backed up by the United States!
Thus in the extreme blue of the South Atlantic,
there're two dolls handcuffed,
fighting, sprouting a global quarrel.

Un desafío

Inglaterra y la Argentina son esposas,
atadas por la larga soga del Atlántico.
Hoy las esposas esposadas
se pelean y bombardean Las Malvinas
buscando datos de posesión,
"Las Malvinas son nuestras",
dice Margaret.
"No, son nuestras",
dice Nicanor.
¡Qué pena!
matan a tantos,
Latinoamérica traicionada,
Inglaterra apoyada,
¡respaldada por los estadounidenses!
así en el extremo azul del sur Atlántico
se encuentran dos muñecas esposadas,
batallándose, creando una riña mundial.

And it's said that meanwhile . . .
(1985)

Mr. Haig implores England
not to humiliate Argentina,
to win and straighten out the quarrel
that disturbs and debilitates the tie
among all the other slaves
of the Organization of American States.
England wins,
Argentina loses.
That's what the press/television tells us in New York.
But
what do Argentinians know?
What do we know here?
Who knows what should be known?
Does truth have a point
where life's reality begins its eternal parade
or is truth
the golden dream of lies?

Y se dice que mientras tanto . . .

El Señor Haig le implora a la Inglaterra
no humille a la Argentina,
que gane y calle la riña
que ya molesta y debilita el lazo
con todos los otros esclavos
de la Organización de Estados Americanos.
Inglaterra gana,
la Argentina pierde.
Así nos dice la prensa/televisión en Nueva York.
¿Pero?
¿Qué sabrá el pueblo argentino?
¿Qué sabemos nosotros aquí?
¿Quién sabe lo que hay que saber?
¿Tiene la verdad un punto
donde principia el eterno desfile de la realidad
o es la verdad
el sueño dorado de la mentira?

Look at Nicaragua
(1985)

Jeanne Kirkpatrick says:
"Nicaragua lives in fear,"
but Nuyoricans know more than that.

Miren a Nicaragua

Jeanne Kirkpatrick dice:
"Nicaragua vive en miedo,"
pero el Nuyorican sabe más que eso.

And in the USA
(State of emergency in New Brunswick, N.J.)
(1985)

If something is not done
Criminal Justice will collapse,
or worse, there will be riots in jails
just like those in Essex, Union and Bergen Counties.
Prisons overflow, they can't hold,
there's no space, the courts dismiss everything,
only extreme cases are retained,
though it's still difficult to hold on to
people who react with brutal crimes.
The hitch is in the rapid dismissals,
can't keep up with those handcuffed,
the courts are jammed,
the list of fugitives grows.
If beds aren't found,
the jails'll explode,
set on fire by inmates
who yield to violent passions.

Y en los EEUU
(Emergencia en New Brunswick, N.J.)

Si no se hace algo inmediatamente,
se desplomará la justicia criminal
o, peor, habrá motines en las cárceles
tal como ha pasado en los condados de Essex,
    Union y Bergen.
Las prisiones se desbordan, no aguantan,
no hay espacio, las cortes despiden todo.
Sólo se quedan con casos extremos
y aún se hace difícil retener
a los que reaccionan con crímenes brutales.
El truco es la rapidez del despacho.
No alcanza a los que esposan,
las cortes se inundan,
la lista de fugitivos se alarga,
si no se encuentran camas
las cárceles explotarán,
incendiadas por los encarcelados,
por los que a la pasión violenta se entregan.

But Jacobo Timmerman knows . . .
(1985)

that Argentina's fighting
the first battles
of the Third World War while
I seek to procure in New York
a direct phone line to Buenos Aires
to know! what to do?
when the quarrel sprouts
and comes close without my seeing it,
although Arabs already peddle in Manhattan
and the Japanese pin Hawaii on themselves
like a tiny electronic candy-bar
jewel in the Pacific,
giving them credit-plans into New York.

Pero Jacobo Timmerman sabe . . .

que en la Argentina pelean
las primeras batallas
de la Tercera Guerra Mundial mientras
yo busco en Nueva York procurarme
una línea telefónica a Buenos Aires
¡para así saber! ¿qué hacer?
cuando el desarreglo se desarrolle
y se acerque sin yo verlo,
aunque ya los árabes venden en Manhattan
y los japoneses se prenden a Hawaii
como un bomboncito electrónico,
una joya en el Pacífico,
dándoles pagos a plazo hacia Nueva York.

Even though . . .
(1985)

Menachem Begin solicits,
and Yasser Arafat mortifies
the biblical peace never found
in an instance never realized,
what can be said when losing?
at not wanting to surrender!
Arafat's trapped, encircled,
and should he count on Ronald Reagan
to break loose with thunder
against Israel, he'll see how frail
this human stay is,
because "Nobody is
      going to
      bring Israel
      to her knees
      . . . Jews
      do not kneel
      but to God."

Aunque ya . . .

Menachem Begin solicita,
y Yasser Arafat mortifica
la paz bíblica nunca encontrada
en un momento no hecho,
¿qué se dice al perder?
¡al no querer rendirse!
Arafat está atrapado, enredado,
y si cuenta con Ronald Reagan
para que rompa a relámpagos
contra Israel, verá lo mortal
de esta temporada humana,
porque "nadie arrodillará
      a Israel.
   . . . Los judios
   no se arrodillan
   sino a Dios".

To My Japanese Readers
(1992)

Yes, I speak of passions.
Yes, I speak of history.
Yes, I short-circuit in love.

And no,
> I do not dislike any part of the globe.

And yes,
> I love what I have seen; both the living and the dying.

And no,
> I do not hate what I have never seen.

What for?
> All there is exists in the doing the daily chores of living.

THE SIDEWALK OF HIGH ART
(1994)

for *Aloud: Voices from the Nuyorican Poets Café*

I. THE SCATTERING OF THE ASHES:
THE BURIAL OF A POET

Many years ago, two poets made a promise to each other, and the promise was deceptively simple. One poet promised the other that by the next evening he would come back with a poem that would lay out in detail what was to be done upon his death.

> Just once before I die
> I want to climb up on a
> tenement sky
> to dream my lungs out till
> I cry
> then scatter my ashes thru
> the Lower East Side.

So it came to pass that Miguel Piñero would die on June 7, 1988. We had been scheduled to do a reading tour of the Southwest, preparations had been made, all our Chicano friends were prepared to feed us menudo for the cruda and taquitos to go along with the tequila.

But that night, Miky did not come home. Miky belonged to the streets, on the concrete and the asphalt of New York, and his disappearances were not rare. It was his operational mode. The streets were where he felt best. It was in the early morning that a phone call came through: Miky had not been reveling and indulging in his excesses but had fallen ill and been admitted to St. Vincent's. My move toward the hospital was automatic, frenetic, and impulsive. I had to look out for my main mellow man, who was both my shadow and my angel.

There's always an eerie silence around the beds of people in intensive care. The only sounds are the electronic machinery insisting on their digital countdowns, insisting with their automatic accuracy how much or how little life is left. Miky's eyes were closed; he seemed deeply asleep, and as I approached him I remember saying to my sister that maybe we ought to wait outside, wait till he wakes, and then we can speak, and then we can visit, and then we can show him our love. But Miky, with that third eye always open to the universe, had in a flash felt my sister's and my presence, and although he could not immediately open his eyes, his fingers moved and his arms twitched, and I knew to enter—that he was conscious and I could speak and be heard, though responses were not to be easily had. I said, "Miky, my love, rest."

I moved toward the bed and put my hand in his, though it was difficult getting to his fingers through the tangle of intravenous lines. He surprised me with the strength of his grasp, and I said, "Tomorrow, we'll leave tomorrow, and if we can't leave tomorrow, we'll reschedule and leave when all is well again." His fingernails had grown long, and his grasp grew tighter and his nails dug into my palm. He wanted to say something, so I tried again: "I'm going to call Jimmy in Albuquerque and tell him that we'll come out next month." He pulled me toward the bed. I saw his eyes slowly open, and his lips barely moved as I bent down and put my ear up to his lips, and he kissed my ear, his hand grasped harder, and he said, "This is our last tour. We must keep all our dates. I will be here when you come back, and anyway, you know what you need to do if I die." I knew exactly what I had to do, and yet I couldn't imagine I would actually have to do it. He seemed impatient with me for staying as long as I did, and he gave me a glance that said everything it had to about my lingering: "Don't you have to catch a plane, Miguel? Why aren't you on your way?" I was shaken, and I knew that I didn't want to leave him. Yet his instructions were very clear.

That afternoon I left for Albuquerque to meet Jimmy Santiago Baca, to enter the holy land of the Chicanos' semiarid, drier-than-dry air and the spiritual world of Quetzalcoatl. The readings went as scheduled. Everywhere I read, everyone was moved and saddened by Miky's absence. His death was announced at 2:30 a.m., June 17, by his brother in a long-distance call from New York. My impulse was to climb on a plane to New York immediately. Miky had, however instructed me to finish the tour, so I left Albuquerque for Taos. A poet's dying will is something that must be enacted and not foiled. So I performed in Taos, got off the stage and into a car, and on my way back to Albuquerque I thought, "I better study my instructions before I arrive in New York." The muscular, now familiar, refrain of the poem kept coming at me; it both refreshed and frightened me. Miky's living will now resided in his verbs:

> So let me sing my song tonight
> let me feel out of sight
> and let all eyes be dry
> when they scatter my ashes thru
> the Lower East Side.

That was my task.

When I arrived in New York, I went immediately to the Wollensky Funeral Parlor, where a great poet lay in state. I knew I was to conduct the ceremonies attendant upon a Nuyorican* poet, which meant that there would be a call let out: "I want musicians,

---

*Nuyorican (nü yor 'ē kən) (New York + Puerto Rican) 1. Originally Puerto Rican epithet for those of Puerto Rican heritage born in New York: their Spanish was different (Spanglish), their way of dress and look were different. They were a stateless people (like most U.S. poets) until the Café became their homeland. 2. After Algarin and Piñero, a proud poet speaking New York Puerto Rican. 3. A denizen of the Nuyorican Poets Café. 4. New York's riches.

I want drummers, and may all the poets come prepared to read, to testify in heightened language to a life lived as a lifelong sonnet." I knew I had to put the poem into action, and I knew that the whole of the community would have to help me lift the poem off the page.

That night Amiri Baraka, Pedro Pietri, Jose-Angel Figueroa, Nancy Mercado, Eddie Figueroa, Julio Dalmau, Amina Baraka, Louis Reyes Rivera, Luis Guzman, and many, many other writers, musicians, and friends showed to celebrate the passing of a man who had left a legacy of poetry and theater behind.

When a poet dies, a whole community is affected, and the Lower East Side was abuzz with despair, sadness, and the keen awareness of the solitude that was coming. We all knew we would no longer see Miky on the streets of the Lower East Side, giving and taking at will whatever and whenever he wanted.

The preparations for the ceremony of the scattering of the ashes forged an unbreakable bond between the artists and the working people of the Lower East Side. Miky had asked that his ashes be scattered

> From Houston to 14th Street
> from Second Avenue to the mighty D

He wanted his ashes scattered where

> the hustlers & suckers meet
> the faggots & freaks will all get
> high
> on the ashes that have been scattered
> thru the Lower East Side.

Miky wanted singing. He didn't want tears. As we prepared the empty lot next to the Café, people came from everywhere to join our procession. A wonderful installation by Arturo Lindsay had been created in that garbage-strewn lot. He had prepared an effigy to be burnt at the site. Drummers surrounded the installation, poets were ready to offer spontaneous testimonials at the installation, and our teacher Jorge Brandon spoke the first words. Brandon, the great master of the oral tradition at the ripe young age of eighty-five, spoke with accuracy and pitch that belied his age and appearance. It was high oratory at its finest. The effigy was lit, and as it burned, a poet stepped up, read a poem, then dropped it into the fire; as that poem burned, another poet would step forward, recite, then drop a poem into the flames. It was clear that Miky's instructions had been letter-perfect. There was simply no other place to start the procession of the scattering of the ashes than the Nuyorican Poets Café, which he had founded with me. The lot was perfect—not manicured, but littered and disheveled and unpretentiously alive. We had cleared only a small circle for the installation, leaving the rest in its natural state: broken glass, strewn brick, unearthed boilers, and local garbage. The poem continued:

> There's no other place for me to be
> there's no other place that I can see
> there's no other town around that
> brings you up or keeps you down
> no food little heat sweeps by
> fancy cars & pimps' bars & juke saloons
> & greasy spoons make my spirits fly
> with my ashes scattered thru the
> Lower East Side . . .

The poem began to leap off the page and become the thing itself—words were becoming action.

I was handed the quart-sized can that contained Miky's ashes. My hands trembled as Joey Castro took the can from me. I asked him to please open it. He pulled out his pocketknife and began to pry the lid gently, respectfully, and yet fearfully. I'll never forget the look on his face when the lid popped lightly and we saw the ashes for the very first time. How very odd—the frame of a man weighs less than two-and-a-half pounds of dust. And what did I have in the quart can? I had the ashes of a man who proclaimed himself to be:

A thief a junkie I've been
committed every known sin
Jews and Gentiles . . . Bums and Men
of style . . . run away child
police shooting wild . . .
mother's futile wails . . . pushers
making sales . . . dope wheelers
& cocaine dealers . . . smoking pot
streets are hot & feed off those who bleed to death . . .

all that's true
all that's true
all that is true
but this ain't no lie
when I ask that my ashes be scattered thru
the Lower East Side.

So the procession left the yard on the west side of the Café and
began its voyage through the Lower East Side in concurrence with
the configuration that the poem had laid out: *From Houston to
14th Street/from Second Avenue to the mighty D*. As we walked, I
would scatter the ashes, and people would say, "Who's that, who
goes there?" The answer would initially come from me, "It's Miky
Piñero." The response would be astounding, "It's Miky Piñero!"
One person would cry out, and then another, "It's Miky Piñero,"
and then another, "It's Miky Piñero." It was a litany, the repetition
of the rosary. People passed the word out in waves of sorrow, com-
municating to each other that the dispersal had begun, that Miky's
ashes were being spread. Piñero was having the burial of his
dreams, his poem breathing, moving and bonding people. By the
time we reached Avenue D the procession was huge. People walk-
ing their dogs, going into stores, and standing at bus stops would
forget the object of their mission and join us. It was as if they were
impelled by a force bigger than themselves. If they were on the
way to work, they didn't go. If they were on their way to the store,
they wouldn't go. If they were going to the park, they didn't go. If
they were walking their dog, they joined us. The murmuring grew

into an audible incantation: "It's Miky Piñero, it's the poet, it's the guy who wrote *Short Eyes*, it's the guy on T.V., on 'Miami Vice,' it's the guy that gave me twenty dollars when I needed it." It was the man that we all knew by many names and in many places.

Great ceremonies are followed by cataclysmic changes. After the procession ended, a great food-and-drink reception had been planned at Roland Legiardi-Laura's loft. The planning for the reception had been spontaneous and exciting. Roland had permitted the use of his place for the send-off of a great poet, and I had found what I was searching for: a big, well-lit space where we could all come to make an offering after the scattering of the ashes. The wake would be accompanied by great food, drink, and recitals. In the midst of this rejoicing, Bob Holman approached me and said, "Miguel, it's time to reopen the Café. This is the moment, you know, and Miky is insisting on it, and we are ready. Let's move on it, let's open the Nuyorican Poets Café again."

Bob Holman's words later began to unravel a need that had been lying dormant in me ever since I had closed the doors of the Café for what had become a prolonged period. Yes, Miky's death was to be a new beginning. From the ashes, life. From the whispered promise made by one poet to another, the oral tradition was to find a permanent home at the Nuyorican Poets Café.

II. THE POETRY OF THE 1990s: FIN DE SIECLE

The philosophy and purpose of the Nuyorican Poets Café has always been to reveal poetry as a living art. Even as the eye scans the lines of a poem, poetry is in flux in the United States. From Baja California to Seattle to Detroit, from the dance clubs with rap lyrics booming to the schools where Gil Scott-Heron plays to the churches where poetry series thrive to community centers with poets-in-residence and coffeehouses throughout the whole of the nation, the spoken word is on fire.

Presidents invite poets to their inaugural platform, and we are now finally paying attention to the need most nations in the world have for a poet laureate: a person who puts into verse the national feelings. Poetry is not *finding* its way; it has found its way back into everyday life. It is not only meaningful, it is also fun. In *New York Newsday*, Patricia Volk has said of the Nuyorican Poets Café, "If you've wondered what effect MTV, the quickness of the city, and life being a vital particle away from death have had on poetry, you'll find out here. The Nuyorican is New York's arena for the spoken word, the poetic counterpart to the second floor of the Whitney Biennial. It's not a floating head above a lectern. It's about getting people excited, about what you say and how you say it. The word is so good, it reminds you that no matter how bizarre life gets, you need poetry."

Poetry at this moment, the last decade of the century, is a growing, developing, challenging force. We have, at the end of the millennium, brought it to life and televised it to the masses. The driving force has been to rekindle the word and the meaning of words. The effort has been to diversify, to turn over mass advertising's dissipation and abuse of language, and to rescue language from the deadening political "isms" that have enveloped it.

The new poetry, or rather the poetry of the nineties, seeks to promote a tolerance and understanding between people. The aim is to dissolve the social, cultural, and political boundaries that generalize the human experience and make it meaningless. The poets at the Café have gone a long way toward changing the so-called black/white dialogue that has been the breeding ground for social, cultural, and political conflict in the United States. It is clear that we now are entering a new era, where the dialogue is multi-ethnic and necessitates a larger field of verbal action to explain the cultural and political reality of North America. Poets have opened the dialogue and entered into new conversations. Their poems now create new metaphors that yield new patterns of trust, creating intercultural links among the many ethnic groups that are not characterized by the simplistic term *black/white dialogue*.

The poets of the Nuyorican Poets Café take responsibility for breaking all boundaries that limit and diminish the impact of their work. It is at the heart of the matter to move their work from the Café into other communities of the city in order to break racial patterns that tend to isolate these communities into ethnic pockets that are enclosed and without intercommunication. After Pete Spiro's play *Howya Doin' Franky Banana* is produced at the Café, it will move to the Frank Silvera Writers' Workshop in Harlem and the Belmont Italian-American Workshop in the Bronx. Thus, the artist becomes a catalyst through which social change is made. It is rewarding when Garland Thompson, the director of the famed Frank Silvera Writers' Workshop, can write to us that "it was a truly exciting new multicultural concept and experiment of yours—to present a provocative new work by a talented white playwright, Pete Spiro, directed by an African-American director, Rome Neal, at the Frank Silvera Workshop, one of Harlem's oldest new playwrights' developmental theatres."

It is clear that there's an urgency among us. We must listen to one another. We must respect one another's habits. And we must start to share the truth and integrity that the voice of the poet so generously provides.

The poet of the nineties is involved in the politics of the movement. There needs be no separation between politics and poetry. The aesthetic that informs the poet is of necessity involved in the social conditions that the people of the world are in. Martin Espada cannot write about the Puerto Rican without identifying the aggression that Puerto Rican people face both on the mainland and in the island. In his poem "Rebellion Is the Circle of a Lover's Hands," he celebrates the fiftieth anniversary of the Ponce Massacre, grounding the memory of people:

> The marchers gathered, Nationalists
> massed beneath the delicate white balconies
> of Marina Street,
> and the colonial governor
> pronounced the order with patrician calm . . .

The order was to repress the peaceful demonstration. The result was a painful bloodletting that remains etched in the consciousness of the Puerto Rican people, Jorge Brandon has been reciting his poem "La Masacre de Ponce" for the last thirty years on the streets of the Lower East Side to anybody who's willing to listen. Brandon's mission has been to say it aloud, to say it on street corners, to say it in the parks of this city, and now, once again, we find Espada, as Brandon, responding to what has been a primary mission of poetry, to inform the living of what has taken place in the past:

> But rebellion
> is the circle of a lover's hands,
> that must keep moving,
> always weaving.

However, the retelling of the stories of the past is not enough. The poet of the nineties has to be responsible for giving a direction, for illuminating a path. It is part of the political and aesthetic responsibility of the oral poet to tell people how to relieve themselves of the anxiety of the day, and it is precisely that task that Bimbo Rivas assigned himself, when he, one of Jorge Brandon's disciples, would exclaim aloud:

> A job
> I NEED A JOB TODAY
> Folks that got a job
> a job that does its job
> can see some sense in this relate
> folks that lost their faith
> that rot away with pain
> DAY AFTER DAY
> Strike at each other
> hoping to find
> in greater pain
> a sedative
> it's all too relative
> my friends
> a man without a JOB
> is lost in the labyrinth of
> HELL.

Bimbo's play on the word JOB—its biblical reference to Job—is clear. If people do not strive to make a change, they will, like Job, remain in eternal pain. The intent is clear. Speak about how people hurt, yet at the same time give them a directive, a sense of future release. The poetry of politics and war, urban war in Bimbo's case, necessitates that the poet tell the tales of the past and that there also be a generous admission: the possibility of hope.

From the battlefields of the inner-city ghettos to the exquisite semiarid landscape of the Black Mesa, the thread of wanting to relate the self to the land upon which one stands runs powerfully and richly. For Jimmy Santiago Baca, talking about the land is not talking about squatting a building on the Lower East Side, but instead moving out into the desert and communing with the earth. So that when Baca says, in his poem "Black Mesa,"

> The northern most U-tip
> of Chihuahua desert
> infuses
> my house
> with its dark shadow,
> and leans my thoughts
> in its direction
> as wind bends a row of trees
> toward it.
>
> I want to visit
> it
> before winter comes . . .

we have a poet seeking the self in the land. Lifting the details of the terrain into the poem reveals the self and shows how the land explains the self to the poet. It is exciting to encounter a Southwestern poet who shows us how rooted in the land he is, much like a mesquite tree is rooted in the earth. Here, the politics of land and people are one, as the poet reinvents the self through the history of the terrain:

> I re-imagine myself here,
> and pant the same breath
> squeezed from these rocks 1000 years ago.

Baca educates himself through his empirical observation of the land. He finds his security in the rocks that lie about. The land is concrete information that feeds the body and the soul and reveals the future. It is an American saga: the land plus people becoming the backbone of America.

In the Northeast, however, the clutter, the vertical living that contrasts so deeply with the horizontal existence of the Southwest, affects the ways in which we bare language, how we peel away its civilities and its decorum, and employ its raw, ribald, coarse, crude, and uncouth imaging. Love and sex are passionately dealt with in the poems of the nineties. The language of poetry is now associated with the great mass of people who are suffering the scathing effects of living so densely together. We cannot ignore how we rape each other, kill each other. Ill-bred and boorish, late-twentieth-century poetic language penetrates the thick urban blight so that Hattie Gossett can talk about "pussy and cash":

> of course there's an endless pool of pussys on reserve waiting for you to
> bring them in
> to run yo household take care of yo kids or grandmama or run yo business
> if you know the secret password—whar da hoz is?—you can get some clean
> freelance pussy to help you through the night when you got to be
> farfarfar away
> from yo regular pussy

The economy of sex goes hand-in-hand with the painful and often mutilating despair that sets in with love gone sour. When love is extended but not returned, the consequences are both scary and despairing. So that when the young girl in Sapphire's poem "in my father's house" serves the meal she's cooked and finds she's not invited to the dining table, she has learned a deep and wounding truth:

> I went to sit down at the table
> & stopped shocked.
> my father had only set a place
> for himself & my little brother.
> "I thought you had already eaten," he offered.
> I made no move to get another plate,
> neither did he.
> he served his son
> the food I had prepared.
> they ate,
> I disappeared,
> like the truth . . .

Love has been offered, and it has neither been received nor returned. The girl has been a tool that provides a meal that bonds father and son but leaves her out and ignored. The nineties are not only a politically unstable decade, but also a period of emotional and spiritual dryness. Still, Pedro Pietri's satirical wit makes us laugh at the total absurdity of the last years of this millennium. He time and again manages to usurp our jaded despair and makes us laugh at ourselves:

> woke up this morning
> feeling excellent
> picked up the telephone
> dialed the number of
> my equal opportunity employer
> to inform him that I will not
> be into work today
> "Are you feeling sick?"
> the boss asked me
> "No, Sir," I replied:
> "I am feeling too good
> to report to work today
> if I feel sick tomorrow
> I will come in early"

The poets at the Café are saying, "Listen, and be aware of the energy and power of words. Do not abandon the self, retain the culture, return to thinking, stop the passive role of the observer, and take up the sport of life."

III. POETRY INTO THE TWENTY-FIRST CENTURY: THE DEMOCRATIZATION OF VERSE

Say it! No ideas but in things. Mr.
Paterson has gone away
to rest and write, Inside the bus one sees
his thoughts sitting and standing. His
thoughts alight and scatter—

Who are these people (how complex
the mathematic) among whom I see myself
in the regularly ordered plateglass of
his thoughts, glimmering before shoes and bicycles?
They walk incommunicado, the
equation is beyond solution, yet
its sense is clear—that they may live
his thought is listed in the Telephone
Directory— . . .

A wonder! A wonder!

    From the ten houses (Alexander) Hamilton saw when he
looked (at the falls!) and kept his counsel, by the middle of
the century—the mills had drawn a heterogeneous popu-
lation. There were in 1870, native born 20,711, which
would of course include children of foreign parents; for-
eign 22,868 of whom 237 were French, 1,420 German,
3,343 English—(Mr. Lambert who later built the Castle
among them), 5,124 Irish, 879 Scotch, 1,360 Hollanders
and 170 Swiss—

                         —William Carlos Williams,
                                 Paterson

    If Janet Jackson had been allowed to follow William Carlos Williams's insight, been able to "Say it! No ideas but in things," her voice would have been the voice of the 1990s and her poetry closer to that of Tracie Morris than to that of Maya Angelou. Jackson's insight into America would have been on target had she been able to say, "So when you wear that gear on your head backwards / it won't make the spot easy / for someone's target practice." But she didn't. She spoke the elegant, often romantic, never less than sonorous language of Maya Angelou. Ms. Angelou's work has been a cornerstone for the development of African-American poetry; however, for *Poetic Justice* to have been the film that it could have been, it would have to have had as its protagonist a woman who talks more like Wanda Coleman, Maggie Estep, or Dael Orlandersmith than the softer verse that speaks of poetry as the "oneness of the human spirit." We are all in a time capsule heading straight into the twenty-first century filled with excitement, writing poems that land on their feet, poems about life's raw edges, correctional institutions, emotional confinement, sexual choices, and regrets. Jackson could have been talking the rough, molten steel of late-nineties verse.

When Alexander Hamilton visited the Falls in Paterson, the population that he found reflected the European immigration to the New World. It is part of Dr. Williams's genius that his epic American poem can exquisitely label with such exactitude the number of French, German, English, Scotch, Dutch, and others who made up the general population around the Falls. These precisely enumerated people were the beginning of what was to become the heart of the American industrial revolution, just as we at the Nuyorican Poets Café, in keeping with the traditions of *Paterson*, open our doors to the multi-ethnic, formally poetic world that comes to us to read, to hear, to be heard. On any night that the doors open for our mock-Olympic Poetry Slams, the magic is in the playfulness of the occasion and the absolute seriousness with which the poets and the audience interact. This is interactive art. If we wanted to make a parallel to the video world, we could call the Slam "Prime Time Interactive Literature."

The Grand Slam starts with our host, Bob Holman, reading his Disclaimer: "We disdain / competition and its ally war / and are fighting for our Lives / and the spinning / of poetry's cocoon of action / in your dailiness, We refuse / to meld the contradictions but / will always walk the razor / for your love. 'The best poet / always loses.'" Judges, who have been selected whimsically from the audience, are introduced with such "qualifications" as being born in Brooklyn or having never been to a Slam before. These judges will rate the poem from zero ("a poem that should never have been written") to ten ("mutual simultaneous orgasm") using the "Dewey decimal rating system" to avoid ties and "the dreaded Sudden-Death Haiku Improv overtime round." Here we are in the realm of literate humor, with no discerning of "high" and "low," all in the service of bringing a new audience to poetry via a form of entertainment meant to tune up fresh ears to the use of language as an art that has been considered dead by many. And after an hour or so of nonstop poetry, our host nods to the deejay in the booth, and the room goes into a frenzy of dance, beer, wine, tea, and coffee, and that's called the Break. Winners go from the Grand Slam to the Nationals, which in 1993 featured poets from twenty-four cities.

The modern Slam is the creation of Marc Smith, who continues his weekly bare-knuckles events at the Green Mill in Chicago. The idea for the Slam grows out of ancient traditions of competitive and/or linked rhymes between orators—from the Greek mythological tale of Apollo and Marsyas to the African griots, from the *Sanjūrokunin sen,* or imaginary poetry team competitions, of tenth-century Japanese court poet Fujiwara no Kinto to the African-American "dozens." It is a tradition that still exists very actively on the island of Puerto Rico, where El Trovador improvises in the plaza, spontaneously pulling into the verse the life of the folks in the small town, the tragedies that have occurred in their families, the gossip that surrounds their private lives, and the celebratory passages that talk about births, deaths, weddings, and baptisms. All of this is compacted into ten-syllable lines with end rhymes. El Trovador moves from town to town in the outskirts of the big cities of the island and is received grandly by the townsfolk, who look forward to regaling him with laughter and drinks when he is entertaining, and/or criticizing and insulting him when he is either too rigid or too drunk to deliver the goods. This tradition of El Trovador coming to perform to the audience for their approval or being punished by their disapproval is totally alive at the Nuyorican Poets Café.

So, it is Grand Slam night, and the slammers are Regie Cabico, Shirley LeFlore, Julie Patton, and Anne Elliott. Our master of ceremonies excites the audience with a short, tight monologue that releases anxiety as it makes people laugh, both at themselves and at the competition that we are about to engage in. Shirley LeFlore, a poet in her fifties, opens the Slam, and with her we enter an almost magical world of Coltrane strains, where LeFlore riffs and talks of Miles, of Armstrong, of Chango, and in her flow she evokes the great poetic jazz tradition of Baraka at his most musical. She comes close to the smooth and angry jazzoetry that has been the characteristic music of African-American poetry of the fifties and early sixties. The crowd is pleased, she is given a warm, enthusiastic response; yet we're all aware of the great tradition from which this comes, and we are clear that her first poem is a tiff away from the pantheon of the likes of Baraka, Jayne Cortez, and Gaylen Kane. The judges weigh in: she is given a 26 out of 30. I am moved by the willingness of the mostly young audience to involve themselves in a poem that is more characteristic of the Greenwich Village jazz-poetic scene than what they have probably come to hear. But who's to say? Chaos at the Café is a blessed state, not a problem.

The second poet, Julie Patton, moves in with long, winding lines that seem to flow along a passive downstream trip into a very private universe where references to Shakespeare and Faulkner and everyday life intermingle in a rhapsodic, seemingly haphazard manner that earns her a 27 for her effort. The poem she has read has been meandering, at times self-indulgent, but the audience hangs in there, following her bravura vocalizations where melody meets meaning. Julie has traveled from a stay at a writers' colony in the state of Washington to be with us tonight. It is exciting that a poet would travel across the country to come to the Nuyorican Poets Café in order to be heard, to be able to stretch out before our legendary young, rowdy, and critical audience.

Regie Cabico, the third slammer, enters the room like a bullet, a young Filipino talking rhapsodically about the "fresh golden fleeces" and the "nine inches" of fun that he desires. Cabico is a dynamo of metaphors spun out of an extraordinarily sensitive blend of gay audacity and Filipino sensibility. By the time that Regie explains "orgasms are onomatopoeia," the crowd is wild, screaming, shouting, talking back to him, involved in his poetic process. Poet and listeners have become one. The room is now the Temple of Poetry. Here we do not exalt it, we bring it down home. We do not lavish praises on the sensibility of the poet, we imbibe him. And then, after we've embraced the poet's daring, we proceed to give him a numerological value. If it seems illogical, it is. If it seems irreverent, it is. If it seems funny, raucous, and vaudevillian, that, too, it is. And the grade that Regie is given is a 29. Regie's delivery has been masterful, controlled, and intense. The excitement builds.

Anne Elliott is our fourth slammer. She has a classic Northern European look, which is an extraordinary contrast to the first three poets' presences. Her projection is melodic, though her verse is a muscular line of thought woven delicately and interlaced with musical accents. She is the "all-new Gregorian chant," as Holman has just characterized her from the stage. The audience has felt at one with his characterization, and indeed it is in sync with what we now begin to hear. Someone from the audience exclaims, "We are in the intestines of a dark devil!" This judgment is anonymous; it is impossible to identify who among the 250 people present has said it, yet it goes directly to the heart of the matter. The silent attention that is being given to her contrasts intensely with the reactive, interactive world that Regie Cabico had created. At the Nuyorican Poets Café, we work by contrasts, and here we are at the extreme of two poetic poles. Elliott is given a 27.4. The audience reacts with an enveloping round of applause, signaling to her a deep appreciation of the mastery with which she's spun the melodic verse and the excitement she created, as if we were in the midst of a sustained passion.

The importance of the Slam, in fact the importance of poetry at the Café, is rooted in its capacity to draw in audiences ranging from our immediate working-class neighbors out for a beer and some fun to serious poetry lovers willing to engage the new poets the Café features to the artists themselves, who seek both exposure of their poems and exposure to other poets. The interrelationship between what has been heretofore thought of as a highbrow art and its appeal to a mass public has become a very important polemic, i.e., poetry seems to want to move into daily American life. The poem, the poet, and the audience grow in a deepening relationship that has become ever more public, ever more popular, and ever more engaging. No matter which way it is seen, it is remarkable to look out into the Nuyorican Poets Café Slam on a Wednesday night or on a Friday night and see young couples sitting, holding hands, embracing, and spending an evening out on the town in a poets' café for no other reason than that it is fun to be here, in this space, involved in this intensely interactive relationship between the poet expressing and the listener absorbing and actively responding. The time has finally arrived when poetry as an interlacing art is being heard from again. It informs, it motivates, it challenges, and it makes for pleasure. It is entertaining. It is a live form of recreation. It couldn't have been said twenty years ago; not even the Beats managed to take poetry out of the coffeehouses. Yet now it is on television, on radio, in the movie houses, and in numberless clubs around the country where live performances of the poem have taken root.

At the center of this movement is "the Largest Stage in the World." On any given night, the master of ceremonies at the Nuyorican Poets Café can look out into the audience and spot the voices that have grown in the room and that have become recognized and beloved by the audience. So when Holman spots Sekou Sundiata in the room and calls him up to perform, the audience is enthusiastic and expectant that Sundiata will deliver a moment of intense pleasure and significant content. If poetry has become a pastime, it is a recreation that actively demands an involvement from the audience to grow, an audience that will seek inside themselves spaces which are unfamiliar to the ordinary ways in which we in the United States find pleasure. When Sekou steps up to the mike, we are suddenly inside a performance that is elevating the discourse in the room: Space, a character from Sundiata's play *The Circle Unbroken is a Hard Bop*, begins to unravel his disjointed view of the world, and we in turn are made familiar with a personage we often run into in the subways and in the streets of the city. Space is a brilliant mind gone awry, having lost all connection to sequential thought. He splatters himself onto the sidewalk, into walls, onto the subway tracks in brilliant metaphoric effusions about how the CIA is taking over his mind, and about his masturbation in the name of Marilyn Monroe. Space's poem is a brilliant insight into what it means to be black, and a self-mocking assault on the audience and the fear that he, Space, can cause in his disjointed world.

Sekou's recital is a great lesson in self-discipline. Inside the play, Space spreads disruptively all over the stage, but before the audience on a Slam night, the character Space is contained inside the poet, and only the words are performed. If the listener has seen the dramatic rendition and contrasts that to this performance, an enormous lesson will have been learned about the theatricalization of poetry, the reason why poetry and theater are so intertwined, and why both are entering into the twenty-first century alive and well at the Nuyorican Poets Café.

Keenness, spontaneity, and trusting the moment are very important for the ceremonial master in the Nuyorican Poets Café. In keeping with the great commitment that the poets at the Café have made to writing the verse on the page and then lifting it off the page into performing action, Holman's eyes survey the crowd, now spotting other poets who have grown in the room. Reg E. Gaines, who entered the room only ten minutes before, is caught and called up to center stage. When Gaines acquires control of the mike, we are in a very special place. Here is an African-American man who has discovered his poetic roots in the voice and sentiments of the Nuyorican poets. Reg E.'s command of Lucky Cien-Fuegos's and Miguel Piñero's poems is astounding. He can, from memory, recite some of their most important poems from the mid-seventies. To recite in two languages is an exciting phenomenon, since it implies that the performer is capable of blending a Spanish verb with an object in English and delivering an impact that excites and arouses the listener.

The fearlessness with which young African-American poets are now confronting languages other than English and involving themselves in the exploration of self-expression in other forms of speech is new and probably the most welcome sign of a new internationalism alive in the young African-American poets. Tracie Morris and Reg E. Gaines do not just make an easy nod to multilingual expression—they are daring in their willingness to stand before live audiences and speak in Spanish. They speak their feelings in Spanish. When Tracie Morris begins her "Morenita" poem, we are soothingly involved and seduced in her bilingual sensual quest for love and precise definitions in relationships. Nuyorican language is no longer the property of Puerto Ricans speaking in a blend of English and Spanish; it is now more like one of the dialects at the edges of the Roman Empire, which were once called vulgar but are now the Spanish, Italian, and Portuguese of modern Europe.

Now, this is the very heart of the matter. They are both attempting complex, intense communications in the Spanish language and are fearless about accents or mispronunciation. They are intent on diving into the endless possibility of multilingual expressiveness. This is new and exciting, and it shows enormous promise for the African-American poetic voice in the Western Hemisphere. Gone are the days when English would remain the only means of expression for North American artists. It is clear that today, alternate systems of speech are growing increasingly popular and creatively alluring. Spanish has been present on the North American continent since the very beginning of the Columbian occupation. It is not about to disappear. In fact, it will continue to grow in importance as the economic relationship between the Southern and the Northern hemispheres begins to equalize.

The linguistic sophistication and complexity grows further when Holman spots Adrienne Su, an Asian-American woman whose simple demeanor and shy presence belie a poet whose sensibility is made of steel and concrete. With Su, the poetic discourse expands beyond issues of language and race into personal moral dilemmas. She approaches the mike and announces that she will read a sestina. When she begins, we're inside a very mild tone, but then the content crosses over, and the audience begins to hear phrases like, "You said the last word with your last / breath and I was not there to bury / it" and "What / you didn't count on was writing / the note, dying, and no one coming to bury / you"; the listener becomes aware of a very powerful statement being made about guilt. Su is saying, "Don't make me feel guilty about your suicide." She finally drives it home when she says, "You intended / to get what you got. Now get out." Asian-American poets have been central to the Café ever since the Basement Workshop and Fay Chiang started to visit us at our 6th Street location. The Asian-American perception of American morality, American culture, and language changed for the Nuyorican poets of the seventies the way in which we talked, the way we used the verb. What was then a relationship of great educational value has grown into an artistic partnership.

The complex moral discourse that Adrienne Su has brought into the room quickly shifts as Bob Holman's keen eye lands on Hal Sirowitz, a poet whose mock-psychiatric plays on family, especially his relationship with his mother, have made his poems extremely popular among Poetry Slam devotees. Everyone is ready and perched for the "Mother said" refrain that Sirowitz has made famous:

> Don't stick your finger in the ketchup bottle,
> Mother said. It might get stuck,
> then you'll have to wait for your father
> to get home to pull it out. He
> won't be happy to find a dirty fingernail
> squirming in the ketchup that he's going to use
> on his hamburger.

Sirowitz's play with depression, repression, psychological tension, and psychiatric outrageousness has made him the late-twentieth-century homespun Sigmund Freud of Slam poetry at the Nuyorican Poets Café. His humor is sharp, and long after you've laughed at what is an apparently simple statement of fact, it keeps on reverberating until you're aware that a great language-smith has been at work. His Jewish-American humor, accompanied by his deadpan delivery, is by now part of the folklore that will be passed on to the twenty-first century.

As Sirowitz takes his applause and the crowd is laughing wildly and madly, Edwin Torres is brought up to the mike, and the crowd is in for yet another mystery tour in the jungle of words that have by now swamped their sensibilities. Edwin Torres, NuyoFuturist, passes beyond all other sound poets and their inventions as he begins to read. Torres depends on the phoneme as the unit of sound. He often begins by hitting a sequence of vowels emitted at an extraordinary range of pitches and volume. This playing with vowels then modulates into vowels accompanied by consonants, and there begin to appear syllables, which stretch from the lower register to the most extreme upper register, a combination of vowel and consonant that leaps between scales and finally can, after a full two or three minutes, reach a point where words begin to appear, not necessarily spoken, but congealing in the ear of the listener, who is surprised by the appearance of a word and then a sequence of words that leads the mind into recognizable sequential language. Is it a stretch? You bet it is. Has it worked? Judging by the audience, who begin to applaud as Torres pulls himself back into familiar noun-verb-object relationships, it has worked. The sound-play begat syllables, which begat words, which begat sentences, which begat a poem.

The poetics that binds these poets is alive and being invented as they themselves evolve as poets and think about their art and their craft. The media coverage that has engulfed these poets has been so plentiful that it is now possible to cull from the endless articles a sense of the poetics that is being created in midair from one article to the other as these poets are made to think about content, quality, and craft. In *Newsweek*, Kevin Powell says, "Poetry is the quickest way to express what you see and feel," yet Paul Beatty seems worried about the hoopla that may dull the critical edge that poetry should have: "The real hook of poetry is that it turns things inside out, and I'm not sure all this trendiness measures with that." Beatty is expressing a very important reservation, but it is a reservation that is not just pertinent to these poets; it is a reservation that is pertinent to anything today in America, where trends are devoured like ice cream cones, in seconds. It is clear that Beatty is worried about permanence and continuity.

Allen Ginsberg recently praised Beatty for "his very smooth, good, sophisticated, syncopated ear." He has also read Beatty's poems as "microchips bursting with information." Ginsberg has once again encapsulated the poetic moment, since it is true that Beatty is a condenser and a fine filtering voice for the experience of the late twentieth century. So that by the time that Evelyn McDonnell in the *Village Voice* describes him as perhaps "the first poet to transcribe the language of the telecommunications age onto paper," we have finally come the full circle round, and we have reached what is probably the best description of the poetics of the first decade of the twenty-first century.

IV. THE OPEN ROOM

The Open Room was the first idea. At the beginning, there was a well-lit, clean, and open space that received the artistic input of anyone who walked in the door, and from this beginning was derived the complex programming that now goes on at the Nuyorican Poets Café. In the early days of the Café (1974–1982), the hosts of the room were mainly Miguel "Lobo" Loperena and Lois Griffith. At the end of the bar, Lobo or I would stand with a ledger and a pencil and simply enter the names of the people who came to perform in order of arrival, so that a famous poet dropping in for the evening could be preceded by a first-time poet and followed by an habitué of the room.

Lobo Loperena would handle the room with his gentle and eagle-eyed capacity to move the room from conversational, social interaction/chaos into a listening audience. This transition was always massively difficult, since it was the practice to have the room filled with recorded music right up to the point at which Lobo would step up to the mike to make that most difficult of all transitions: taking people from muscle-body-action (dancing) to mental-ear-repose (listening).

It still remains a magic memory for all of the people present on the night when Lobo stepped up to the mike and, in an effort to make a dramatic transition from recorded music to poetry, announced that the poets of the Nuyorican Poets Café had created a Nuyorican chant. He then proceeded, for the first time ever, to perform what was to become the classic chant for our poetry performances and for the room:

La	La	La
Le	Le	Le-e-e-e
Le	Le	Le-e-e-e
Le-e-e-e-a!		

Tru cu tum
Cu tum cu tum
     {clave:///}

Tru cu tum
Cu tum cu tum
     {clave:///}

Pa' eso te pulla
Pa' eso te duerme
Lo mio no es violencia
Lo mio es dulce

La	La	La
Le	Le	Le-e-e-e
Le	Le	Le-e-e-e
Le-e-e-e-a!		

And the first poet is . . .

The deep chest-tone and the sustained vowels of the chant galvanized the audience, which had been sweating and frantically moving to the music; within seconds, Lobo had managed to make the dancers into listeners. He had found a way to move from dance to poetry successfully. The room filled with a cathartic round of applause. Instead of the usual begrudging attitude often accompanied by boos, which heretofore had preceded such a transition, the audience yielded to what was the room's mission after all, the performance of poetry.

The Open Room had found its ceremonial master in Lobo, and Lobo had found that his Nuyorican chant became an inspirational and practical way to move people into a space where self-expression and poetry can take place.

The Open Room is a gathering place for all kinds of writers and readers who are, for the most part, jittery and anxious about the moment that is coming to them. The poets wait for their names to be called, poems tightly gripped in hand. They are ready to face the audience. It is an audience that is not ready to bear the weight of boredom easily, and people who sign up know that the result can be either crushing or elevating.

The Open Room is the basis for the open, generous, embracing attitude that is, in fact, the aesthetic of the Café, and its continuity through all the years is our root. The Open Room simply must happen every week, since the opportunity to come back the next week is what gives the poets the impetus to write that next poem and allows them to learn how to relax through the nervousness that distorted or destroyed the poem the week before.

It is important that poets know they can always come back the next week, that the audience will be there, supportive or critical but never passive, hungry for the images that the poets have found in the interim. For example, one of the regular poets of the Open Room is Pauly Arroyo. Pauly has been with the Nuyorican Poets Café from the very beginning. In the early days, he was a martial artist who would get up and perform martial art katas for the Open Room. It was fascinating and riveting to watch Pauly masterfully exhibit the physical control of breath and body as he performed his katas. The audience would go wild, and approval would be his. As the years passed, Pauly moved in the direction of language and began reciting verse. This met with very critical responses from the audience, often disappointing Pauly, yet week after week he would return, challenging himself and the audience again, and the outcome has been an engrossing evolution in which Pauly has reached a place where he can combine his martial arts movements, display his virtuoso control of breath, and engage language that can stir and animate the audience. He has finally arrived at a performance where breath, physical movement, and language have come together, and the audience has given him the recognition that he's wanted. He is becoming a poet who can express experience and arouse the listener:

> And though we play our tunes
> the ghetto still plays the sound with us
> we bongo like madness we bongo our dreams we bongo our tunes

don't let us be stopped because we won't we will keep tryin'
and if we are still a rhythm of sound
let our music bounce from every wall and town
and if we can play the tune once more
I'll play it just for you.

While Pauly Arroyo's development in the room has been progressive and has incorporated many elements, Shorty Bón Bón's poem became a classic hit in the room from the very first moment that he recited it. It was a rainy night, and Shorty came into the room looking for shelter, looking for warmth, and looking for love. I remember spotting him and instantly went to the ledger and entered his name. When it came time to introduce him, he was still sopping wet with a glass of wine in one hand, a cigarette in the other, and a poem in his mind. The poem was "A Junkie's Heaven," and once he recited it, the room went wild and requests for a repeat began immediately; in fact, it might have been the first time that the room as a whole asked for a poem to be repeated. Shorty obliged and felt proud at the reception of his poem and at the birth of a Loisaida* classic.

His sacrifice was not in vain
though he died because of an abscessed
brain
a junkie dreamt
of his lament
When I die
I shall go to a land
where the cocaine is clean
and I'll smoke my pot only when it's
at the darkest of green
here all the angels are junkies
and the Christ is so hip

---

* **Loisaida** (lō ē ˈsī da) (the Lower East Side in Nuyorican, a creation of Bimbo Rivas) 1. That portion of Manhattan stretching from "Houston to 14th Street/From Second Avenue to the mighty D,"—Miguel Piñero. 2. The eternally transitional neighborhood known in other incarnations as the Lower East Side (see Ed Sanders's "The Yiddish-Speaking Socialists of the Lower East Side" and "The Low East" {David Henderson}). Also check out the street signs along Avenue C, "Loisaida Avenue," and Bimbo's mural on C between 5th and 6th.

that for the crime of my bootlegged
wine
he'll demand two sips
yes, come to my heaven where all
the junkies walk free . . . and
remember all you potheads out
there
the smoke is on me . . .

The Open Room has become the trial ground for "slammers"
to practice away from the blinding spotlight of the Friday night
Poetry Slams. The greater calm and ease of the Open Room can
and does give space for people to discover their poems, to hone
their work, and, since the room is so receptive, poets often go for
issues that are close to their hearts or issues that are inspired by
political current affairs. These Headline Rhymes are direct, wet-
ink-on-the-page responses, the news told as an individual's
response, not a committee's decision. Like the poets of the sixties
and seventies told of Vietnam and Cambodia, here you will hear of
the War in the Gulf, the Los Angeles riots, natural disasters of all
types, and serial killers. Often, too, the personal and political inter-
sect, and you will hear poems on rape, whether it be the reporting
of a rape or the autobiographical revelation of the experience.
Oftentimes, it seems as if the mind of New York is on display and
that the mind of the poet and the city are one in their concerns.

Carol Diehl takes the question of women and men and their
relationships out into the audience in a semiserious comic release
that drives the Open Room audience crazy:

What if
        the ability to menstruate
        was the prerequisite for most high-paying jobs
....
What if
        women were always making jokes
        about how ugly penises are
        and how bad sperm tastes

Since someone in the audience or at the bar will always inform the poet, "We can't hear you," one of the most precious Open Room lessons that the young poet can learn is how to react to a heckle, how to use the mike, how to acquire calm and poise, how to improve the recitation of the poem. The Open Room is where a "virgin" poet takes the first steps to becoming a performing poet. Sometimes, however, a "birthday poem," a poet's first poem, is his or her last. Nevertheless, most poets are willing to come and share. in the nerve-racking wait for their names to be called and then face the audience's reaction. You never know who might be in that audience, and it is part of the charm of the Open Room night that many people have found friendship and companionship as they come back week after week seeking people who are listening to others speak.

After reading, a poet can relax and enjoy the heartfelt congratulations, sometimes even receiving an invitation to read in another place. Many poets have gotten their start in the reading circuits around the city in the Café's Open Room. Of course, there is always in the Open Room the opportunity to make an absolute fool of oneself and not have to worry about it, since there is a sense of communion and connection and great partnership that comes from a reading that takes place at 2:00 a.m.

To be a host of the Open Room, as in the great tradition of Miguel "Lobo" Loperena, you have to have a great sense of balance, the capacity to absorb constant heckling and interruptions of people going to get wine, beer, coffee, and tea, and the sound of people booing, jeering, or approving a poem. The room is in constant flux. The host must be a very centered person. Lois Griffith has been at the heart of the Open Room for the last decade. Now, Keith Roach has evolved into the quintessential Open Room host, capable of handling the readers, the audience, and the feel and flow of the room. As Keith says, "It happens, on occasion, that there is a poet who is overwhelmed and done in by the moment. Sometimes, vapor lock occurs. These are some of the most engaging moments. Someone will step forward and restore some of the poet's lost dignity. Most poets who undergo this experience realize that there is some more work, some more practice, some more nerve." The success of a great Open Room night lies squarely on the shoulders of the host's resourcefulness, inventiveness, and generosity. The evening's master of ceremonies carries the full weight of the night's success.

And finally, the Open Room contains an ambience so rich in the folklore of Loisaida that readers with national and international reputations have stepped in as surprise guest readers to enjoy themselves, the room, the bawdy atmosphere, and in so doing, by their very presence, they always incite the crowd and heighten the performance of the Open Room devotees. All you can be assured of at the Open Room is surprise, poetry in all stages of gestation, and a simpatico crowd in the wee morning hours.

Proem
II
(1997)

Infirmities take over the body without warning or proclamation. The potential for infection is endless and the capacity for the body to restrain and combat the armies of trillions of cells that would destroy the biological balance and health of the body is, at best, limited. Very often, the body's defenses are helpless.

We have known the power of plagues from the beginning of time. It is not new to die by the hundreds of thousands. It is often hunger that claims whole populations. However, in the late twentieth century, it is not hunger alone that is responsible for mass death, but viruses. These viruses have a capacity for mutating so rapidly that medication is rendered useless before it can successfully treat the symptoms or help the body retrieve its innate fighting capacity. In the face of this biological warfare, we must devise a moral field that defines our behavior towards each other. There are plagues carried by the air—in those cases, we quarantine the bearer. There are, on the other hand, plagues that can be controlled if we use personal restraint and care in how we meet to share love with each other.

HIV
(1994)

I.
Revelation
To tell in strength. "The telling," when to tell, leads to a discovery between the teller and the listener. Acquiring knowledge; the teller holds his/her information as a tool for health, movement towards truth.

II.
Salvation
To converse as an attempt to recuperate, a holding on not to die.

III.
Speech
To acquire "language" for talking about a plague in the self.

IV.
Sharing Secrets
Who to tell? Is there someone? The search for what to tell.

V.
Mature Masculinity
Welcome the responsibility to do the work of building verbs, adjectives and nouns for mortality and its subsequent eternal breaking of concrete.

> I.   *Revelation*
> Revel at ion,
> rebel at I on a course
> to regret erections,

to whip the cream in my scrotum
till it hardens into unsweetened,
unsafe revved elations
of milk turned sour
by the human body,
of propagation of destruction.
The epiphany: I am unsafe,
you who want me
know that I who want you,
harbor the bitter balm of defeat.

II.   *Salvation*
If I were to show you
how to continue holding on,
I would not kiss you,
I would not mix my fluids with yours,
for your salvation
cannot bear the live weight
of your sharing liquids with me.

III.   *Language*
To tell,
to talk,
to tongue into sounds
how I would cleanse you with urine,
how my tasting tongue would wash your body,
how my saliva and sperm would bloat you,
to touch you in our lovemaking
and not tell you
would amount to murder,
to talk about how to language this
so that you would still languish
in my unsafe arms and die,
seems beyond me,

I would almost rather lie
but my tongue muscle moves involuntarily
to tell of the danger in me.

IV.   *Of Health*
To use my full and willing
body to reveal and speak
the strength that I impart
without fear,
without killing,
without taking away what I would give,
to use my man's tongue
to share,
to give,
to lend,
to exact nothing,
to receive all things,
to expand my macho
and let the whole world
into the safety of my mature masculinity.

V.   *Quarantine*
Sometimes I fear touching your plump ear lobes,
I might contaminate you.
Sometimes I refuse odors that would
drive my hands to open your thick thighs.
Sometimes closing my ears to your voice
wrenches my stomach and I vomit to calm wanting.
Can it be that I am the bearer of plagues?
Am I poison to desire?
Do I have to deny yearning for firm full flesh
so that I'll not kill what I love?
No juices can flow 'tween you and me.
Quicksand will suck me in.

Father at Zero-Point-Place
(1994)

I

My mother's pleading voice, not resigned,
sang a crying song wishing for a rebirth,
my uncle, weeping for the first time
in my memory, sobbed,
"His eyes are open he's still looking at me,
you better get over here I don't know what
to do, we've lost him."
I transformed each telephone word
into concrete objects:
I was there looking at father's soft skin,
touching his gentle lips,
caressing his still warm hands and fingers,
craving for a breath to escape him,
tricking myself into feeling his air
pressing on my cheek,
running my hands over his body,
looking for the warm spots,
his belly's hot,
his armpits still lukewarm,
his thighs, grown so thin, beginning to be cold,
my hands grab at his feet,
not yet icy cold,
I run my hands into his groin,
and there I find body heat, I find
his scrotum still simmers with an
amber temperature, his penis still
holds a glow, his buttocks

are now room temperature,
there is still a chance for a revival.
His eyes involuntarily open,
will he stand up and walk
among the sinners and the ill?
Will he continue to walk the earth beautified
spreading saintliness
just as he had during my youth?
a kinder man lived only in books,
father's feather-weight touch
opened all of us to a fault,
because nowhere else were we ever loved
so gently and so fairly,
he was a judge with mercy and kindliness
in his heart
and understanding and balance were his law,
he knew that at the heart of law was generosity
and that mercy made human contracts work,
here was a Daniel, a Solomon,
a worthy homespun philosopher of family justice.
Yes, there is still a chance for a revival,
the rebirth that takes place in the mind.

II
I've already found my Deep-Space Nine photograph,
but mother spins an endless reel,
she cannot stop to cradle a single frame,
she keeps on running the tape
of her fifty-seven years with him,
re-playing their never having slept a single night apart,
the reel to real joy of eternally
rejuvenating happiness in married partnership,
the video of never having been lonely,
or alone or without her man,
without his warming her slippers

so that they wouldn't be cold to her feet,
or his cooking her special diet to cure her ulcer,
or his buttoning her blouse
or pulling up her zipper,
his patience with her mental break-ups,
or the way in which he crossed his legs
when company arrived,
but the reel that drives mother hauntingly wild
is the empty bed, life without him,
even the seventy-five pound
more fragile than frail body
that his wasted frame had become was her man
still there, needing his pillows,
her hand to brush his teeth,
his feces cleaned and removed,
needing his enemas, needing his spit suctioned,
needing his liquid food,
cleaning his intestinal tube
through which travels medication and nourishment,
yes, that's the real reel,
the non-occupied space,
the zero-point-place,
the nobody in space and place,
that's the terror Uncle Al
experienced this morning,
that's the tremor that rocked mother,
they both awoke hoping a dream had passed
that the zero-point nobody-in-place-space
had evaporated, that father's
more fragile than frail body
would still be there.

III
Mother and Uncle Al
arose hoping that the police

had not been there,
that the death certificate
had not been signed,
hoping that the body
had not been picked up
by the La Paz Funeral Parlor embalmer,
who made a southbound turn
onto the northbound traffic on Queens Boulevard
with my father's cadaver
neatly tucked into a body bag
in the rear of his station wagon
which I was following,
furiously blowing my horn,
waving my hands,
screaming, whistling,
frantically blinking my lights,
fearing a collision
that would catapult father's corpse
unceremoniously into the chill, rainy night air,
a flying body bag and me,
my old man
doing triple somersaults
in the midst of his encroaching rigor mortis,
finally, the embalmer, dazed by the oncoming headlights,
crossed over the median divider,
stopped at the red light,
looked over at me, shrugged, and said,
"Hey, he's at zero-point-place
and nothing else can get at him,
only the great blaze
shines on him now,
he's at homeplate and safe,"
then the light turned green
and my father and the embalmer
drove off into the pure white light of forever.

Proem
I
(1997)

Angels are human interactions with the incorporeal world. Sometimes it seems as if the angel is an object outside the body that is transforming internal time and space into a metaphysical thunderstorm. However, more often it is the possession of the body by biological changes in pulse rate, blood pressure and oxygen levels that can make you levitate internally, while the state of mind possessing you whips your limbs and innards into a frenzy. Angels are sometimes people, objects or simply live-wire ideas. The connection with this world of direct electricity can be controlled in part by letting go of the self in order to let the typhoon through, tidying up internal space afterwards.

Nuyorican Angel Voice
(1997)

Little Jimmy Scott speaks music,
stringing his lyrics together,
never has any angel heard him sing a melody,
"All of me,
why not take all of me."
Jimmy talks his passion by hitting the syllables
the joy of sweat on limbs becoming one blood flow
"That's deeper than the deep blue sea is,"
you see
"that's how deep it goes if it's real
but if you let me love you
it's for sure I'm gonna love you
all the way."
Never just a melody,
always hitting the feeling,
androgyny never existed except in someone's body,
if it's a question of *"all the way,*
only a fool can say,"
without being loved all the way,
yes! *"all the way,"*
'til *"day by day"* we make it deeper by far
than any ocean,
I am wider than your hold can take,
but I'm yours to stay
through the years
"day by day"
you're making all my dreams come true,

all the way to where I am yours alone
yes, I am yours to stay,
'til you understand how much I love you
and those mourning roses
I've sprinkled with tears,
how I've traveled to be where you are,
how long is the journey from here to your star
and if I ever lose you
how much would I cry
"just how deep is the ocean
how high is the sky,"
 just how long is the suffering
yes, *"how deep is the ocean,*
how high is the sky,"
before seeing you gets hazy
and a gentle touch turns hard.

Japanese Nuyorican Angel
("I Don't Want to Busy My Desires")
(1997)

No, I don't want to busy my desires,
I'll just hold a stone
to feel an embrace,
too much of anything
is not happiness.
I must say
stop
and not busy my desires.

Nuyorican Angel Papo
(The Bi-Sexual Super Macho)
(1997)

I.
The Fourth of July fireworks
went unseen by me.
If you could not see them
then I would not see
the New York skyline
ablaze in colored fire.
The red, white and blue
would climb to the moon
without my Fourth of July
Coney Island, Bushwick, Brooklyn
churchgoing,
newfound friend,
we parted in the name of fear,
the not falling into the black hole
of speedy passions
and underdeveloped love.
I drove you home,
shook your hand as we opened the trunk
to get your pack,
but you know, really,
I almost pushed you back
into the car, the hearth,
the fireplace of warmth,
the wheels that would have,
could have crossed the Williamsburg Bridge,

into Loisaida,
driven us into a nest of dreams
and corruption,
and purity and cleanliness
entwined in next to perfect lust,
yet, no, instead,
I didn't see the fireworks.
Instead, I sat thinking about
how nice it was to have left you
without our rushed desires fueling
the blazing Fourth of July skyline of New York.

II.
I tried
to separate
where we should start to touch.
I tried postponing, first with "Straight out of Brooklyn,"
then food,
but you were on an impulse
to burn fire, to scorch passions,
I should've left you in Bushwick,
without numbers exchanged,
I could have lied about my name,
yet could have and would have
live in conditional tenements,
where on the third floor
we committed unconditional love,
knee-to-knee
nude from the waist down,
lust-fueled hands full
of belly buttons, buttocks and meat.

Nuyorican Angel of Euthanasia
(1997)

I. Serial Killer Angel

I was thirteen when I first
molested a young boy.
Then I began to kill.
I once stabbed one,
didn't realize it though.
I didn't know my knife had entered.
Later I found out it penetrated the stomach.
I fantasized about it everywhere,
even at work I just thought about
going to a school, a movie, a park,
it's what I wanted to do,
assault, rape, abuse young boys.
I am on death row,
if you want to let me out,
go ahead, but outside I'll just
keep doing it, within hours I'll
be after one, it's what I want to do.
If you set me free,
it's what I'm going to do,
so you might as well hang me,
or if you want, let me out,
but once out there I'll do what I want to do,
I'll kill another one.

II. Angel of Mercy

The rope prepared according
to State Department specifications
snapped his neck neatly.
The specs called for a specific knot
that would not let him linger,
it broke him like a twig.
His victims hadn't been so surgically killed,
his was a carefully planned suicide,
it wasn't justice, not really,
it was a man demanding to be killed
not out of remorse but a dare,
"Don't kill me and I'll do it again."
He staged his own suicide,
no ACLU eager esquire,
no madcap campaign against Capital Punishment
could stop him from throwing his glove down,
could stop his slap in the face,
his "I want to die and the State of Washington
will have to build a gallows and a trap door
'cause if it don't,
I'll do it again"
So you see, in the way of things,
in the round of peeling oranges,
he hung himself,
though he made the State
prepare the noose,
he committed legal suicide,
at the hands of the long arm
of a trap-door-pulling justice of the law.

For J. R.
(1997)

When I realized I loved you,
it was too late to take your hand out,
wrench it from the grip it had on my heart,
I would have spurned your bed,
spat on your face.
Instead I fell
like a stupid yo-yo
right to the end of my rope,
without rebound to climb
up that cotton thread
back to myself,
where I could've fought you off,
never letting on that I couldn't move
without holding on
to your firm alabaster body,
never letting you know
that it was not glamorous
to dream of white limbs
spread-eagled over my brown body,
wrong, it was wrong,
white on brown should be left
to Skippy Peanut Butter
on White Wonder Bread.

Proem
III
(1997)

From Delancey to 14th Street, from Third Avenue to the FDR Drive, lies the neighborhood known as Loisaida. Tens of languages are spoken on literally every block. And, though covered by tar and concrete, the yards of our tenement houses are filled with bushes, flowers and fruit trees.

Loisaida has changed much. In the 1950s, when I was a child, my mother had me fetch our daily quart of milk from the dairy storefront run by Mr. Schervina. He in turn got his milk from the back of the store, where he kept his ten milk-cows. Walking down Avenue C, I could inhale the smells of the Italian food-stands, and then pick some fruit from the open-air fruit stall. On Orchard Street, I watched the clothes vendors carry their wares on horse-drawn carriages, and then later the horses walk unhitched in teams of twenty back to their stables. On Sundays I liked to observe the Jews and Puerto Ricans, who traveled to the blintz-shops on First Avenue, where they ordered matzoh-ball soup and drank tea served in glasses with a wedge of lemon.

While things have changed since then, we residents of Loisaida still cook homemade jams and share them with our neighbors and lovers. Once lost love is often rediscovered here in our barrio. Loisaida is our home, a place to mourn the loss of the major players on the streets of Loisaida, who too often fall to plagues, violence or killing.

Proem
IV
(1997)

We come into the world naked, nurtured and protected because the world around us can devour us physically and mentally. We are helpless, in need of support, caresses, and kisses. It takes a long time for a human being to be self-sufficient and capable of self-defense.

We also begin our life at the same time that we begin to die. Biological attacks and deterioration happen from the inside out. As we come into our greatest mental and physical form, we also start the downgrade into old age and deterioration. Facing this, we embrace life in order to meet death in our private historical landscape, our sense of the immortal "I AM?"

Bimbo's Young Son
(1997)

Driving my '76 Buick Electra 225
past Tina's house, I see wreaths and lit candles,
facilitating the path for spirits rapidly departing.
A child is running 'round the grieving mother's knees,
the child is hopscotch jumping 'round
lit candles on the sidewalk,
"Don't put them out," the grandmother warns,
while the child talks to the light,
"My daddy, my daddy's there,
in those candles,
in those lights?"
Tina grabs her grandchild by the shoulder,
pulls his tiny limbs towards her
and asks, "who told you?
                Who talked about it?"
The child answers calmly and possessed,
"I see him and that's my dad
and he's dead, look at the lights,
look, you see, he's in there."
I kiss Tina and she asks me,
"How did he know, how did he find out?"
I give no answer,
but invite her to our vigil tonight.

Hillebrand Funeral Parlor,
Woodhaven Boulevard
(1997)

Some mourners bear their pain behind delicate smiles,
others irrigate their loss
with voluminous cataracts of tears.
But my father's family arrived carrying
brown paper bags filled with memories,
vodka, cranberry juice,
and other losing preparations
that shorten life and lengthen pain.

We probably should've stayed
in the Bronx,
but mother preferred
"a more classical environment"
for father's farewell,
a kind of upscale, white stucco walls,
Hollywood cornices, wall-to-wall
acrylic parlor.

Yet heart-to-heart feelings
fill the Naugahyde vinyl room
that could have made father's
death a plastic jubilee.

Father was simple, clean,
transparent, irrepressibly patient,
no absence of humility or love
in him,

he was blessed at birth
and during his stay he shared
a life of love, no surprises, even in his death
there were no surprises.

He lived as cleanly as he loved.
Father may you enter
the kingdom of clean, clear,
unfettered living,
may a pure trumpet tone announce
your entrance into translucent space.

Michael Skolnick
(1997)

I.

Time past, time present,
time future, you and I,
we used to, in time past,
count syllables, check on end-rhymes,
diagnose language directed to body/listener,
chemical exposure to grammar,
nothing, no thing,
like two men telling stories
in rhymed verse to each other.
Michael, in time past,
we were joined at the ear
and shared a common blood flow,
now, suddenly, you are time future,
damn how could I have known
I'd be time present,
you time past and future,
Michael, you better start whispering
the whereabouts of the spirits
from your vantage point.
They have got to be playing numbers
and hovering over Adela's restaurant on Avenue C
waiting for closing time
to collect leftover food
for homeless Angels residing in Tompkins Square Park.
Oh Michael remember how we read
Hamlet and *The Merchant of Venice*,
together in time present,

but now, you're past and future in one
and I'm left out,
alone, once more.

II.

How could I have known
that I'd arrive early at
Riverside–Gramercy Chapels,
how could I have known the aggression
of the chapel attendant,
        "You're early, too early,"
how could I have known you're to be seen at six
and that I'd get there at five,
how could I have known I'd be late for your
earliness,
that your name thundering in my ears
would be Gabriel's trumpet
announcing to the world
that you now counsel the Lord,
Yahweh, that He is now getting
some of the best advice Heaven can get,
how could I have known
that Bob Rosenthal would be in tears,
when I telephoned for your number,
years had passed, seasons had gone and come
but your name thundered in my mind
Monday night.
Tuesday morning, from my office,
where you and I used to talk
about literature, Richie, Marilyn,
Kathy, and my Siamese cats,
Tuesday, I called you because you rained
upon me like a monsoon of memories,
Tuesday, when I called for you Bob wept,
and well, Michael, how could I have known.

Alvin Ascends
(1997)

When the procession has arrived,
I will sing to you,
the choir will sing to you,
the angels will do double arabesques
and all the sky will sparkle
with hands and feet stretched
to touch your departing mantle.
Max Roach will play vibrant dark drum rolls
as the procession moves its funereal beat
slowly,
very slowly,
Arthur Mitchell, Tally Beatty,
George Faison, Gary de Loatch,
Keith McDaniels, Marilyn, Mari,
all moving slowly, Roach playing los palitos,
composed, denying overt tears,
Butler, Premice,
Mrs. Cooper held,
Chenault Spence lighting Alvin's path,
designing at this very moment
a yellow, white road for the Master's next move,
Judith Jamison more striking and balanced than ever,
David Dinkins poised to lead New York
in an invitation to the Lord to lift our Alvin,
on high, for his is the resurrection,
        the life,
and as Alvin believed,

and as Alvin's eyes beheld Him,
and as he created for Him,
Alvin shall never die.
With nothing he came
With no thing he leaves,
he saw our holy world
revealed through gospel music,
he reworked and made old things new,
"it is done my Lord, and now I am your son,"
said Alvin, as he twisted torsos
into a praising of the Lord, begging Him to
        fix me, Jesus, fix me,
        fix me for my errant ways,
        fix me, Jesus, fix me,
        for I've Been 'Buked and Scorned'
        and talked about from shore to shore,
        so fix me, Jesus, fix me,
        and as you know that day by day,
        by legions we all die Lord,
        and since you know, O Lord,
        that We've Been 'Buked and Scorned'
        fix us, Jesus, fix us
and Jesus does fix,
Jesus fixes when Ashford and Simpson
sing goodbye to you Alvin,
Jesus fixes when Judith exhorts
Alvin as her spiritual leader
who made her believe that she could fly,
        that she could cry,
        and by the time
        that she had danced his cry
Alvin would ask her "What now?"
After the bravos, the screaming adulation,
the hollering audience, after the triumph

she'd find that Alvin had already moved
          to that empty space
where Judith would have to travel again
          with her spiritual walker,
knowing she would have to cry anew
not because she would die
but because she would be born again
          in another dance,
yielding up the secrets of her heart to him,
again, over, again, over, again.
Alvin will not shut his eyes and ears
O Lord, immortal Creator and Maker of Man,
give rest, O Christ, to your Servant Alvin,
let him go down to dust
where sorrow and pain are no more,
where the days and nights are past and gone, O Lord,
          rocka-his-soul in the bosom of Abraham,
          rocka-his-soul in the bosom of Abraham,
          rocka-his-soul in the bosom of Abraham,
and let him remain with you for all time,
listen, Lord, to Roberta Flack loving Alvin always,
listen, Lord, to Max Roach,
listen to Max for his drums are the last pulse
before Alvin's ascension,
listen, O Lord, to how the cymbals announce
his arrival at your house,
listen to his simple knock,
no fanfare, just a worker Lord,
a suppliant choreographer knocking at your door.

Lucky CienFuegos
(The Man of a Hundred Fires)
(1997)

I. Lucky Talks

Don't cry when I die,
It's not pain, it's a setting forth,
no tears can wash away my smell,
so forget the liquid rush,
and get some words to say
how I held time in my veins,
pulsating, digressing, begetting,
regretting, embedding
noun-verb-object
relationships into my coffin,
don't cry, just tie a knot
of words whereby I won't forget
you still remember.

II. Lucky's Presence

No sectioned, spliced genetic slide
can tell how he smoked, walked, gulped,
talked 'bout women 'tween their thighs,
expert he,
        on how they slid towards
his ultimate instrument of intrusion,
that which penetrates all ego,
leaving fuming, moistened dreams
of mucous film on blood-stretched skin
made hard by male desire.

III. The Fires Are Extinguished

So what if you're dead,
I'm here, you're gone,
and I'm left alone
to watch how time betrays,
and we die slow
        so very slow,
we talked of sharing time
beyond quadruple-heart-bypass
and non-clotting-blood
that spills like your last breath forever,
without stoppage,
no heartbeat in you my friend,
no pulse, I fear I'm all alone.

On Seeing Miky's Body
(7th Street and Avenue A)
(1997)

What the hell are you
doing in there?
Your lips sewn,
your eyelids shut
            for
                ever.
What do you think you're doing
hidden in that casket?
Come out, come on out
and let's play,
what's a guy to do
without you, without CienFuegos,
without his main mellow man?
Who's a guy to play with?
Make words with.
Got to get you back!
How come you let me go,
didn't I love you
with the right "e"?
Not the one for empty,
not the one for enough,
but the one for eternally,
like I'm eternally yours,
you eternally mine,
but now, now you can't
come play with me

in Tompkins Square Park,
and I can't get mad at you?
Figure that one out!
Who am I going to be mad at?
Damn you take a lot of liberties
leaving me in Loisaida
with all my planets atwirl,
silly like a spinning child,
swirling and straining,
and crying too,
like the day I was chasing you
in Tompkins Square Park
to make you stop saying
what you were saying about me,
I don't remember now
what it was you were saying,
but I skinned my knee
trying to catch up to you
and what would I have done
had I caught up to you
except shake you and hug you
and jump into our usual jump-rope,
just you, me, and Lucky skipping,
twirling the rope faster and faster
till we could shout at him
"you're out,"
at which point Lucky would say,
"it beez that way sometimes
and even after I die,
it'll be that way always."

Sublime
(2008)

Sublime
The world is beauty,
seek it, trust it,
move towards balance,
yield to its harmony,
its peace, its pleasure,
sublime, sublimity,
above the highest,
on a par with God,
the Highest Power,
or the self alone
looking for perfection,
hold fast,
don't fold,
open senses to all input,
leave room for fast-forward,
take advantage of roots sown as a child
in this very neighborhood,
in this small island, in this Loisaida,
in this tiny corner of the world,
of the globe, of the planet,
plan your entrance
into Heaven,
into God's garden,
into this ghetto of gold and silver flowers,
soon you'll see
the whole of self,
not part, but its entirety.

A CONVERSATION WITH
MIGUEL ALGARIN

You were born in Puerto Rico but grew up in New York City. When did you arrive in New York City and what was the transition like?

In 1951, July 3rd, I'll never forget when the plane door opened and the sunshine came in. All of a sudden night had daylight. I, my sister and younger brother were permitted off first. Mother, Father and Uncle Al followed carrying suitcases filled with clothes and shoes that would no longer be of service to us. Clearly, we could have left all we carried behind. The "new world" welcomed us and we were ready with enough to survive a short six weeks.

How would you describe your relationship to Puerto Rico? Did you visit the island frequently as a child? Do you have family there?

I always have had family on the island. There were long periods of adjustment for the subsequent groupings of our folks as they left the island of Puerto Rico and slipped into the island of Manhattan. I did not visit the island frequently as a child, but as I came into my twenties I began to make frequent visits to vacation on the island and to see my relatives.

How old were you when you began to consider yourself a writer? Was there one person or event that stands out as having influenced your writing?

I do not "think" of myself as a writer. I do know that my relationship to language is strong. Verbs have always stuck close to me. I've always thought of myself as a verb. In fact, there are T-shirts that have a line from a poem of mine that blare: "I am a verb."

Could you describe what it felt like to be onstage at the Nuyorican Poet's Café in the early years?

Standing on stage at the Nuyorican Poets Café as the lights went down felt like the spotlight of truth was denuding my feelings, making my tongue the messenger of truth. The attempt to speak was always an attempt at simplicity and clarity. I didn't always hit the verbs on the head but the effort, the desire to communicate was always there. To fail at making contact was always humiliating.

When writing, do you consider how a poem will be delivered to an audience: heard as a live performance or read in solitude?

The poem and the audience are always in the instance. Failure to couple talk to ears scrapes the skin and bloodies the poet. Solitude is for the dead. A poem is always scratching for performance, a reading, an airing.

Could you explain why music seems to be a recurring motif in your poems?

Music is a recurring motif in all poems. My poems are always seeking tones that enliven, sounds that ground the poems in the synapses of the reader. Music in the poems are the life-line to eternity.

Much of your work deals with political strife both in the United States and abroad. What prompted you to become politically engaged?

Politics is life. Life is poetry. The politics of poetry are the incidences that tie the writer and the poems to a particular, recent or actual occurrence.

In addition to writing poetry, you also write plays. Do the themes that appear in your poetry show up in your plays? How do you decide if the seed for an idea should grow into a poem or a play?

All of my theatrical work comes from the world of experience that is the ground; the conflict that is found in the poetry. Poems are plays, conflicts that grow into scenes.

How did a Nuyorican poet become a professor specializing in Shakespeare?

Shakespeare loves conflict. Nuyoricans live in eternal tension, looking to understand the daily toll of living. Shakespeare looked into those corners of pain more than any other writer. So where else should a Nuyorican look except to the master technician of pain.

What are you working on now?

I am finalizing a four-volume work called "Dirty Beauty." It will be my last book of poems before moving on to a collection of short stories.

CHECK OUT OTHER POETRY COLLECTIONS
FROM ARTE PÚBLICO PRESS

Body Bee Calling from the 21st Century
Miguel Algarin
1982, Trade Paperback, ISBN-13: 978-0-934770-17-0, $7.00

"*Body Bee Calling from the 21st Century* turned me on after exhibiting beauty and gentility, miraculous writings from the Lower East Side of New York."　　　　　　　　　　　　　　　—Allen Ginsberg

Time's Now / Ya es tiempo
Miguel Algarin
1985, Trade Paperback, ISBN-13: 978-0-934770-33-0, $7.00

Winner, 1985 Before Columbus Foundation American Book Award

The Other Man Was Me: A Voyage to the New World
Rafael Campo
1994, Trade Paperback, ISBN-13: 978-1-55885-111-5, $8.00

Winner, 1993 National Poetry Series Open Competition

From the Cables of Genocide: Poems on Love and Hunger
Lorna Dee Cervantes
1991, Trade Paperback, ISBN-13: 978-1-55885-033-0, $7.00

Winner, 1992 Paterson Poetry Prize, and *Winner, 1993 Latino Literature Prize*

Terms of Survival
Judith Ortiz Cofer
1995 (Second Edition), Trade Paperback, ISBN-13: 978-1-55885-079-8, $7.00

"*Terms of Survival* takes readers on an imagistic safari through the lush jungle of life . . . [it] is a slim volume that is sure to grab the reader's interest from the first page to the last."　　　　　—*The Athens Observer*

Palabras de mediodía / Noon Words
Lucha Corpi
English translation by Catherine Rodríguez-Nieto
2001, Trade Paperback, ISBN-13: 978-1-55885-322-5, $12.95

"Corpi's first book of poetry, *Palabras de Mediodía* (1980), is a document of the immigrant experience, of an inevitable yearning for home, and of desires to record a new existence as a mother and an independent woman . . . a welcome addition.   *—COUNTERPOISE*

How to Undress a Cop
Sarah Cortez
2000, Trade Paperback, ISBN-13: 978-1-55885-301-0, $9.95

Winner, 1999 PEN Texas Literary Award

"There will always be room on the shelf for 'How To' guides of this nature."   *—Kirkus Reviews*

Bluestown Mockingbird Mambo
Sandra María Esteves
1990, Trade Paperback, ISBN-13: 978-1-55885-017-0, $7.00

"Esteves speaks with punch and politically-astute vigor about the realities of the urban poor. More importantly, however, the poetry draws a big distinction between one being economically poor and spiritually and culturally repressed."   *—Poetry Flash*

Some Clarifications y otros poemas
Javier O. Huerta
2007, Trade Paperback, ISBN-13: 978-1-55885-500-7, $10.95

Winner, University of California, Irvine's 2005 Chicano/Latino Literary Prize

"If you're in the mood for language that poses riddles of identity, that rides on the heat of its own melting, pick up a copy of *Some Clarifications y otros poemas*. You won't be disappointed."
     —Southwestern American Literature

AmeRícan
Tato Laviera
2003, Trade Paperback, ISBN-13: 978-1-55885-395-9, $11.95

"*AmeRícan* is branching out, the striking of sympathetic chords with other cultural groups on the basis of expansive Puerto Rican sound and rhythms."   *—Journal of Ethnic Studies*

Enclave

Tato Laviera
1981, Trade Paperback, ISBN-13: 978-0-934770-11-8, $7.00

Winner, 1981 Before Columbus Foundation American Book Award

La Carreta Made a U-Turn
Tato Laviera
1992, Trade Paperback, ISBN-13: 978-1-55885-064-4, $7.00

"[This is] a clear and refreshing note of affirmation, humaneness, joy and vigor in the face of poverty, alienation and oppression. Tato Laviera has produced a remarkably varied first book of poems."
—Explorations in Ethnic Studies

Mainstream Ethics
Tato Laviera
1988, Trade Paperback, ISBN-13: 978-0-934770-90-3, $7.00

Mixturao and Other Poems
Tato Laviera
2008, Trade Paperback, ISBN-13: 978-1-55885-524-3, $12.95

"Laviera challenges the idea of the purity of any language, as both languages, English and Spanish, are transformed by non-European elements. Thus the 'AO' . . . becomes the linguistic symbol for . . . resistance to acculturation [which] reside(s) in the African component of Puerto Rican culture, on the Island and in the metropolis." *—CENTRO Journal*

Promesas: Geography of the Impossible
Gloria Vando
1993, Trade Paperback, ISBN-13: 978-1-55885-059-0, $8.00

"These intense poems explode like flares about a battlefield of the heart to reveal a geography of the impossible." *—Library Journal*

Shadows & Supposes
Gloria Vando
2002, Trade Paperback, ISBN-13: 978-1-55885-360-7, $11.95

Winner, 2003 Latino Literary Award—Best Poetry Book

"Intelligent, crafted, compassionate, with a sharp eye for the absurd and the unjust, the poetry of Gloria Vando should be savored like a good meal." —Martín Espada, author of *City of Coughing and Dead Radiators: Poems*